MULTIFUND INVESTING

How to Build a
High Performance Portfolio
of Mutual Funds

MULTIFUND INVESTING

How to Build a High Performance Portfolio of Mutual Funds

Michael D. Hirsch

DOW JONES-IRWIN
Homewood, Illinois 60430

© DOW JONES-IRWIN, 1987

ISBN 0-87094-912-8

Library of Congress Catalog Card No. 86-71215

Printed in the United States of America

5 6 7 8 9 0 B 4 3 2 1 0 9 8

To Dad, rest in peace, for taking me into a stock brokerage office when I was twelve.

To Mom, for being Mom.

And most important, to my anchor, Janie.

Michael Hirsch has successfully brought back the "fund of funds" concept. He has quietly but methodically introduced his Mutual Funds Investment Program to a broad section of investors across the country, including his own trust customers at the Republic National Bank of New York. The numbers tell the story: meaningful participation in rising markets resulting in an excellent cushion during periods of weakness.

The growing complexity and ever-increasing volatility of the financial markets combine to support the Hirsch approach as one alternative strategy for money management. The program has the ability to incorporate diversification of market sectors, investment styles, and individual issues into a single, cost-effective investment approach.

One important characteristic of this fund of funds approach is its focus on long-term performance and away from the self-destructive, short-term performance derby that promotes security and manager turnover. This is an investment approach that appears to disprove the misguided notion that investing in stocks and bonds for incremental returns is a losing proposition.

Both novices and investment experts will find Hirsch's book stimulating and educational. The novice will quickly learn about the growing complexity of financial markets and force himself to evaluate his own investment goals and risk parameters. The professional will find a methodology and strategy that is unique and, perhaps, compatible with his own investment management organization. Happy reading and investing to all.

Richard B. Hume, CFA

PREFACE _____

There is something drastically wrong with the investment markets. Irreversible changes are taking place that
have created significant dislocations for both individual
investors and professionals. A recently released study
reveals that over the past two years the number of individual shareowners has declined by 3 percent. This re-
verses an ever upward trend in individual shareowners
since the end of World War II. Although the past two
years have been a favorable period for the stock market,
small investors obviously feel at a disadvantage in attempting to cope with today's tumultuous marketplace.

Nor has the environment treated professional investors any more kindly. As *Business Week* pointed out in the
featured article of its February 4, 1985, issue—"Why
Money Managers Don't Do Better"—only 44 percent of
professional equity managers were able to top the 14.8
percent return of the Standard & Poor's 500 Stock Average for the 10-year period that ended in 1984. When over
50 percent of these managers fail to match market returns, how can these full-time professionals claim to be
providing a value-added service to their clients—often at
quite substantial fees? And if professionals are experiencing so much difficulty, what chance do individuals have in
approaching the process on their own?

In every sector of the investment industry, signs of
upheaval are apparent. Bank trust departments, whose
share of the pension management business has shrunk
by some 30 percent over the last five years, have in

many cases shut down their internal investment management function and are now purchasing this capability from outside sources. Many once highly regarded money managers no longer provide an active management capability, instead, they now offer indexed, or passive, products. Many brokerage firms are suggesting the services of independent investment managers to their larger clients instead of making individual buy-and-sell recommendations themselves. Many corporations have dedicated a substantial portion of their large corporate retirement plans to core investments, such as index products and guaranteed investment contracts (GICs). Such retirement plans allot only a small percentage of plan assets to managers who can supposedly provide a value-added service.

All these trends seem to imply that "the game is getting away from the players," that it is no longer possible to beat the market. Many look at the stock and bond markets today and conclude that the situation is overly treacherous. Although historically stocks and bonds have provided returns in excess of such supposedly secure investments as bank deposits, the risks to many appear to outweigh the rewards. And so does the advent of passive investing and other defeatist approaches.

This book will convey my strong belief, which is based on over 11 years of experience, that it is premature to throw in the towel. There is no reason to forsake those historical incremental returns because of a misguided notion that investing in the markets has become a losing proposition. Far from it! Since 1975 multifund investing has been successfully tried and tested, not on paper and not through some computer simulation, but with actual accounts totaling in the millions of dollars.

What differentiates this approach from more traditional investment methods is apparent from the book's title. By following the method described in these pages, not one penny of an investor's money will go into direct investment in a single share of stock or a single bond. Mutual funds will comprise the *entire* portfolio. As we shall see, a carefully constructed multifund portfolio of no more than 10 to 20 select funds will provide the investor— whether an average individual or a sophisticated professional—with all the necessary ingredients for success in today's treacherous environment.

How much success? Through this approach investors with a balanced objective, that is, those seeking both growth and income, have achieved over the 11 years that ended in December 1985 compound annual returns of *15.4 percent;* there was *never* a losing year! These returns were consistent and above average. Even investors with a maximum growth objective experienced a loss in only three years. In no single year was the loss greater than 4 percent. The record speaks for itself.

The question I often face, therefore, is, "If it works so well, why isn't everyone doing it? It seems so simple and straightforward." I must admit that this is a difficult question to answer because the evidence seems to be overwhelmingly favorable. One can only conjecture. My best guess is as follows: most individual investors and all institutional investors, including banks, insurance companies, and investment counselors, are so imbued with the idea of direct investments in stocks and bonds that they have never considered mutual funds as an alternative. But as we shall see in Chapter Five, a growing number of both individual and institutional investors have begun to consider funds as an alternative means of investing. Professional investors face the additional problem of having an entrenched investment department with which to cope. If you accept the premise set forth in this book, what do you do with all your security and bond analysts, portfolio managers, and support staff whose services are no longer necessary when you take the mutual fund approach? Having worked with many banks around the United States to install this investment system, I can assure you that there is a most satisfactory answer to this question. (We'll discuss it in Chapter Eight.)

Another reason why the mutual fund approach is not used by a wider audience lies with the mutual fund industry itself. In the 1950s and 1960s when the marketing of mutual funds intensified, the thrust was directed at the small, unsophisticated investor. The pitch was simple: if you don't have the time, expertise, or sufficient capital to invest on your own, then buy mutual funds. The inverse message was implied but clear: if you are sophisticated, if you have a large pool of capital, you don't need to invest in mutual funds.

So, by the industry's own actions, most substantial individual investors and practically all professional investors never bothered to look at mutual funds as a viable alternative. This book will attempt to cure those misconceptions. For I strongly believe that the only possible route to consistently satisfactory investment results in an increasingly volatile and complex environment is through multifund investing. I am not talking about one fund, or two or three funds selected at random, but rather about the precise portfolio-building process described in the pages that follow.

At this point let me explain the organization of *Multifund Investing: How to Build a High-Performance Portfolio of Mutual Funds*. Part One—The New Marketplace—states the book's central thesis: my belief that the basic composition of the investment markets has gone through drastic changes within an amazingly short time. These changes are identified as volatility and complexity. We will explore their characteristics in depth as well as the impact they have on the traditional style of stock and bond investing. My conclusion is that the current highly complex and volatile investment environment is not conducive to the traditional approach.

Part Two—The Investment Vehicle for the New Marketplace—takes up the open-ended mutual fund, which I regard as the ideal answer to the changes described in Part One. The open-ended fund has been available as an investment vehicle for the past 45 years. But because of misunderstandings and a lack of information, it has not been used effectively until recently. Part Two also looks at the inherent strengths of mutual funds: their liquidity, efficiency, and flexibility. These characteristics make mutual funds the ultimate form of investment for our current environment.

Part Three—Multifund Investing—examines the unique features of multifund investing, including the simple, straightforward procedure to follow in assembling a cohesive portfolio of mutual funds. (A word of caution is necessary here: I strongly recommend that you study Parts One and Two before turning to Part Three.) We next look at the ability of multifund investing to deliver consistent, above average returns, regardless of the market environment. We explore in depth its exceptional safety and risk-avoiding features: its triple safety net. We describe how to assemble a multifund portfolio and how to monitor it efficiently. In fact, as you will see, both the assembling and monitoring require only a fraction of the time you would normally spend on such tasks under the traditional approach. We will also refute some objections to multifund investing: the pyramiding of fees, the delegation of responsibility, and the system of closet indexing.

In a word, all investors—both individuals and professional investors—can benefit from the features offered by individual funds as well as from the strengths inherent in the multifund portfolio. In this way investors will have the advantages of a multimanager, multistyle approach. People formerly excluded from the advantages of the most advanced, state-of-the-art investment techniques can now profit from them. In addition, investors already using the multimanager approach, such as the sponsors of large pension plans, can benefit from multifund investing.

I have attempted to make this book accessible to readers at all levels—from first-time investors to senior investment officers of multimillion dollar institutions. I believe that all of them might benefit from these ideas. If at times the writing seems below or above your level of sophistication, please forgive me. It is not easy to address such a diverse audience. Because I have spoken on this subject to many different people, including individual investors, financial planners, bank trust officers, and retirement plan officials, I have strong reason to think that there is a vast potential audience for this message. Whatever your level of interest in investing, whatever your sophistication or past experience, this book will stimulate your thinking. Enjoy it!

Michael D. Hirsch

ACKNOWLEDGMENTS

When one holds down a demanding full-time job and is, therefore, writing his first book on a part-time basis, there are many people to be thanked for their encouragement, support, and assistance.

Thanks to my dear friend, Professor Larry Robbins of The Wharton School, who helped me to stay on the right track, and who saved me immeasurable time and trouble through his terse commentary on my drafts.

To my loyal staff: Robin Lee Bilkis, Maria Cordero, Oswaldo Costa, Adrienne Doobin, Anne Kazazis, Rachel Levenberg, Mary Lustig, and Guy Sebeo; I want to express my gratitude for their help in information gathering, typing, copying, collating, seeing to countless details, and, most importantly, for being so understanding.

Thanks to Erick Kanter, Lisa Swaimann, and the entire research staff at the Investment Company Institute for their invaluable assistance in putting together the basic research on the mutual fund industry, and to Steve Leuthold and the entire research department at Salomon Brothers Inc. for helping gather the background material on stock and bond market trends.

I must thank my two guiding lights in the institution I work for, Edmond Safra and Jeffrey Keil, for their foresight and perspicacity, and for having nurtured a creative environment in which multifund investing could flourish and grow.

Last, but definitely not least, thanks to my most

treasured possession, my family, Jane, Daniel, Jill, and Joseph, for putting up with months of having an absentee husband and father.

To all of you, thank you from the bottom of my heart.

M.D.H.

CONTENTS

The Investment Pyramid. The Proper Emphasis. Two
Teams of Specialists: Portfolio Managers and Mutual
Fund Managers.

PART ONE

The New Marketplace

CHAPTER ONE

The Problem of Volatility

In a little over 10 years the investment markets for stocks, bonds, and currencies have gone through some truly significant changes. Because of the nature of these changes, a new set of investment principles must now be followed. What has aggravated the situation is the fact that the time span of these changes has been so short that market participants have not had a chance to react adequately to the new situation. Furthermore, two major problems—volatility and complexity—have developed at virtually the same time, compounding the investors' difficulties in coping with these changes even further. We will discuss volatility first.

THE SITUATION PRIOR TO 1970

To appreciate the impact of volatility on the marketplace we need to recall the environment in the decades after World War II. It was then common dogma that the stock market took from three and a half to five years to complete a cycle. (A cycle is measured from a low point to a high point, and then on to a new low point; conversely, a cycle can be measured from a high point to a low point, and then on to a new high point.) Within such a time frame an investor has sufficient time to absorb developments, analyze them, decide how they will affect investments, modify strategies, and make the requisite changes in his or her portfolio structure.

It was, therefore, quite sensible to create broadly diversified portfolios consisting of perhaps 40 to 50 stocks, 15 to 20 bonds, and perhaps half a dozen short-term cash instruments. Such diversification significantly reduced portfolio risk. An investor who owned only 1 stock was at much greater risk than the investor who owned 10 stocks. Given the pace at which the markets moved prior to 1970, there was usually sufficient time to keep track of and periodically alter the mix of these many holdings; one could truly be in control of the portfolio. The unsophisticated investor, peering over this wide variety of holdings, at times might have been perplexed by the complex mixture of stocks and bonds, but the portfolio served its purpose of attempting to attain the desired investment objectives with as little risk as possible.

THE TRANSITIONAL PERIOD

After 1970 the whole situation changed. Stock market cycles were no longer measured in terms of years. The measuring rod today is—quite literally—a matter of weeks or even of days. The time frame has not been slightly shortened; instead, it has been so dramatically compacted that it bears little or no resemblance to the past experience. A few examples will illustrate this point.

The first indication of the new reality came about during the plunge of 1973–74, which was followed by an equally dramatic market rise in 1975. Not only was the scope of the decline noteworthy but the manner in which it developed was also unusual. Of course, the market had experienced substantial declines in the past, but none had shown such short-term ferocity.

Steven C. Leuthold, an astute market observer, conducted an in-depth analysis that showed just how volatile the marketplace became during this period. According to his measuring rod, any day on which the Dow Jones Industrial Average (DJIA) rose or fell by more than 2 percent would be considered a "high volatility day." Leuthold reported that "over the last two and three quarter years, 1973 through the third quarter of 1975, there have been 69 high volatility days with moves of 2 percent or more (38 up days and 31 down days). This compares with a total of only 57 high volatility days *in the entire 24-*

year period from December 31, 1948, through December 31, 1972 (24 up days and 33 down days)."[1]

The fact that the total of up days and down days was in virtual balance over this period belies the argument that such volatility was symptomatic of everyone's trying to sell at the same time. Volatility occurred almost as frequently on strongly upward-moving days. Also, we cannot write off this new experience as symptomatic only of the 1973–74 bear market and the ensuing 1975 bull market. During the prior 24-year period equally significant market thrusts had occurred in 1957, 1962, 1966, and 1969–70. But none of those markets had had the volatile characteristics of the 1973–75 cycle.

The next significant experience began on Thursday, August 12, 1982, when the Dow Jones Industrial Average closed at its lowest point for the year: 776.92. (This was also its lowest level in the prior 27 months.) Overall, the economic news in the weeks prior to that date had been negative. The fraud at Penn Square Bank of Oklahoma City was discovered; the largest subsidiary of Banco Ambrosiano of Milan defaulted on *$400 million* of indebtedness;[2] consumer prices were still rising at double-digit rates; and quarterly corporate profits were at their lowest levels in five years. On July 21, the Federal Reserve Board announced that it would stick to tight monetary targets. One week later, on July 28, President Ronald Reagan predicted that any forthcoming economic recovery would be slow. On Monday, August 9, newspapers

---

[1] Steven C. Leuthold, "The Causes (and Cures?) of Market Volatility," *Journal of Portfolio Management* (Winter 1976), p. 21.

[2] As this book is being written, lawsuits and investigations are still in progress over these two cases of fraud, malfeasance, and scandal. All of the perpetrators have yet to be brought to justice.

around the United States reported that corporate purchasing managers were extremely pessimistic over the future course of the economy. And on that very day—August 12—a major government bond trading firm, Lombard-Wall of New York City, failed.

Supposedly level-headed market technicians and strategists were caught up in the gloom. The previous Friday, August 6, one analyst was quoted as saying, "We're in a bear market, and it looks like we're going lower." Another market expert was reported as saying on August 11, "The market acts like more bad news is coming." Overall, the mood on Wall Street was very pessimistic.

The only ray of hope in all this gloom was a number of steps taken by the Federal Reserve Board (the Fed). On July 19 it lowered the discount rate (the rate charged to member banks) from 12 to 11.5 percent. Eleven days later on July 30, this rate was slashed once again to 11 percent. With admittedly perfect hindsight we can now point out that a trigger event for the market occurred on August 13 when the central bank cut this key rate for a third time in less than a month to 10.5 percent. Without the benefit of such hindsight, yet another respected market observer was quoted as saying on the following Monday, August 16, "The Dow may plunge to 640."

Despite such "sage" advice, the market began to rise on August 13, and in *seven* trading days went from its low point of the year to its high point. Literally half a cycle in one week's time! Along the way some other interesting records were set. On Tuesday, August 17, the Dow Jones Industrial Average rose 38.81 to 831.24, making it the single largest daily advance since that average was first kept. The following day the volume of trading on the New York Stock Exchange totaled 132.7 million shares, the first time a daily volume had ever exceeded 100 million shares. The market had effectively demonstrated that it could change its complexion in a matter of days.

The rally went on and on and on. It did not stop until the Dow Jones Industrial Average had risen by over 80 percent in approximately nine months. And the advance was less than orderly. The volatility that first appeared on August 13 resurfaced time and again in the following months. In fact, between August and December 1982, the DJIA rose by more than 10 points on 54 separate days—more than half of all trading days during that period—and during those five months it had an average daily price change of 11½ points![3]

While there was a halt to the rally in 1983—a year that had an inconsequential second half—the curse of heightened volatility was still apparent. In 1971 the average daily price change in the DJIA had been 4.47 points, and there were 22 days on which the DJIA had moved up or down by more than 10 points. By 1983 the average daily price change had expanded by almost double to 8.20 points, and there were 82 days on which the DJIA had moved by more than 10 points.[4] One year later, in 1984, a new level of volatility was reached that by comparison far overshadowed even the explosive days of 1973–74 and 1982–83.

Almost two years to the day after the start of the 1982–83 advance, volatility struck again. Although the 1982 rally had occurred within a basically negative economic atmosphere, the 1984 rally began when the economic recovery was at its height. But because of the jitters that accompany such sharp, short market movements, investors feared there might be an unseen black lining to the silver cloud. If the economy became "too strong," they believed, the Federal Reserve would have to

[3] Jane A. Staunton, *Institutional Holdings—1982* (New York: Salomon Brothers, 1983).

[4] Laszlo Birinyi, Jr., and Jody E. Needle, *Equity Market Review and Outlook—1983–84* (New York: Salomon Brothers, 1984).

tighten the money supply, causing interest rates to rise and thereby slowing or halting the recovery.

Again the ray of hope came from the Fed. Speaking to a Congressional committee on July 24, 1984, Paul Volcker, chairman of the Federal Reserve Board, announced that current readings of the economy did not seem to show any reason for the Fed to tighten its monetary policy. At once the debt markets reacted favorably, but the stock market remained stalled. Because of the experience of the previous two years, such hesitancy might appear justified.

And once again many market strategists misread the signals. Here are a few examples: on Thursday, July 19 (as the market slid 8.72 to 1,102.92), one analyst remarked, "I don't see a reversal soon. . . . This isn't a good-looking market." The next day, following a further 1.55 point decline, a second expert stated, "This isn't just a correction; this is a bear market." On Thursday, July 26 (the second consecutive day on which the DJIA rose by more than 10 points to 1,107.55), a third expert opined, "Analysts doubt that the rally can be sustained. . . . [It's only] a technical rebound." Lastly, there occurred an almost perfect carbon copy of a similarly mistimed forecast in 1982. On Wednesday, August 1, as the market soared 19.33 points to 1,134.61, yet another analyst commented, "The market could possibly go as high as 1,140–50. . . . [This] rally could be short-lived."

The trigger events this time were two negative economic announcements. On Wednesday, August 1, the government announced that the leading economic indicators were down 0.9 percent and that factory orders had dropped 1.4 percent in June. The logic that seemed to be clearly emerging on Wall Street was as follows: If the economy was, in fact, weakening, the Fed would not be forced to tighten the money supply. This was exactly what Chairman Volcker had testified a week earlier. The ensu-

TABLE 1-1   Rise in Dow Jones Industrial Average,
July 30–August 6, 1984

Date	DJIA	Point Change	Volume (millions of shares)
July 30	1,109.98	− 4.64	72.3
July 31	1,115.28	+ 5.30	86.9
August 1	1,134.61	+ 19.33	127.5
August 2	1,166.08	+ 31.47	172.8
August 3	1,202.08	+ 36.00	236.6
August 6 (Monday)	1,202.88	+ 0.88	203.1

ing uproar, as depicted in Table 1–1, dwarfed all that had transpired in the history of organized stock markets.

The week of July 30 to August 3 was record-shattering in many ways. The gain in the DJIA for the week (+87.46) topped all previous weekly totals; the volume totals on both Thursday (August 2) and Friday (August 3) smashed previous one-day totals by a wide margin; and Friday's total of 4,784 block trades of 10,000 shares or more set a one-day record for that barometer of activity as well. Most important, that advance finally laid to rest any lingering hopes that at some point the market would return to the "good old days" of long, drawn-out cycles. For here we had the antithesis of such a prediction: an extraordinary one-week market, both in terms of scope (696.1 million shares traded) and direction (+87.46 points). Only in the perverse atmosphere that now permeates the marketplace could negative news trigger such positive developments!

Those analysts who wrote off the 1973–74 experience as an aberration should have been quieted down by the 1982–83 market. If this was not so, the 1984 advance would have dramatically confirmed their worst fears. The following joke circulated among U.S. money managers (with more than just a touch of black humor): "If you were on vacation during the first week of August, you missed the market!"

As Table 1–1 indicates, even though the huge one-day volume totals continued for one more day into the following week, the rally had ended. There was no carryover. However, as in 1982, the symptoms of a heightened volatility persisted during the ensuing months. But instead of double-digit daily changes in the Dow Jones Industrial Average, as was the case in 1982, we now had the advent of the "one-day rally." Four separate times in the next six months—on August 9, October 18, and December 18 of 1984, and on January 21, 1985—the DJIA rose from 28 to 35 points on a single day. In each instance the market action both on the day preceding and the day following the eruption was mediocre at best. An article in the *New York Times* quoted a leading Wall Street figure as saying, "It's just a characteristic of the market in this day and age. All the moves are very compressed, and what used to take a week to accomplish happens in a day."[5]

TODAY'S SITUATION

By the mid-1980s the new time frame of the marketplace was firmly established. Rallies and declines would transpire rapidly and an extremely large volume of shares would trade hands. What events or parties were responsible for this dramatic change? Who or what had so altered the very nature of the stock market?

The facts point strongly to institutions: private investment counseling firms, trust banks, insurance companies, and mutual funds. The managers of hundreds of

---

[5]Michael Blumstein, "One-Day Rallies Perplexing Traders," *New York Times,* January 28, 1985. The individual quoted in the article is John A. Conlon, Jr., head of equity block trading at E. F. Hutton & Co.

billions of dollars of assets for individuals and retirement plans were capable of transacting 4,784 trades of 10,000 shares or more within a single day.

An inkling of the extent to which these mega-investors would affect the markets of the future first surfaced in the early 1970s. In 1971 the Securities and Exchange Commission delivered to the 92nd Congress an eight-volume study of the growing impact of institutions. The conclusions of the study were rather mild. Nothing close to what would actually transpire over the next decade and a half was alluded to in the study. The presence of such large investors was recognized and their potential power was admitted, but the consequences were glossed over.

Another in-depth study issued the previous year by an equally prestigious body—the Twentieth Century Fund—reached approximately the same conclusion:

> Thus, there does not appear to be any noteworthy trend in market efficiency from the 1958–1960 to 1967–1968 periods in spite of the greatly increased stock activity by institutional investors over these years. . . . The concentration of power over portfolio companies (corporations whose shares are owned by the institution) implicit in the growth of a number of giant organizations oriented toward equity investment has been a basis for concern totally apart from the other economic implications of the growth in institutional equity investment. . . . We do not feel that this danger is sufficiently great to warrant restrictions on the size of institutional investors at this time, though perhaps restrictions on the amount of investment in stock of individual portfolio companies by institutions other than mutual funds may be in order.[6]

---

[6] Irwin Friend, Marshall Blume, and Jean Crockett, *Mutual Funds and Other Institutional Investors* (New York: McGraw-Hill, 1970), pp. 93–97.

Clearly, here is another case of an inability to foresee the institutional tidal wave that would shortly swamp the investment markets.

Exactly how does institutional style trading change the tone of the markets? A marketplace with 1,000 participants, each trading an average of 100 shares, will be more stable and orderly than one in which there are only 10 participants, each trading in 10,000 share units. This is because of the depth provided by the larger number of participants. Now extend that simple example to the current state of affairs. Today there are literally thousands of institutional investors capable of purchasing or selling 50,000 to 100,000 shares of a single issue in a single order. When a large percentage of these institutions are all buying or all selling 50,000 to 100,000 share blocks at the same time, you have the elements of a disruptive situation. Such concentrated purchasing or selling power is the source of the current volatility.

Leuthold aptly described the situation in these words:

> The market structure mechanism (dealers and specialists) cannot be expected, from a capital standpoint, to counter a position against large institutional orders. . . . If a dealer does, in fact, take down a large block as inventory, chances are it will involve a significant price concession, thus increasing market volatility. Selling short into a large institutional buy order is akin to financial hari-kari. . . . In summary, the institutional market of recent years has, to a large degree, destroyed the cushion effect (provided by the specialists in the old days of diverse, smaller orders) out of individual stock price fluctuations.[7]

Until now, we have examined the institutional influence on markets as a whole. We shall soon look at institu-

---

[7]Steven C. Leuthold, "Short-Term Volatility: Causes, Effects, and the Implications," *Pensions & Investments,* June 9, 1975.

tional influence on individual issues. Figure 1–1 shows the extent to which institutions took over the market between 1978 and 1984. If we were to carry the data back even further, we would find that for the 10-year period 1975–84, block trades (that is, trades by institutions) as a percent of total volume on the New York Stock Exchange (NYSE) grew from a mere 15.6 to 49.3 percent, or close to one half of all trades![8]

In heightened periods of activity, such as during the two consecutive days—Friday, August 3, and Monday, August 6, 1984—when volume exceeded 200 million shares each day, it has been estimated that institutional activity accounted for over 90 percent of the total. By May 31, 1985, Salomon Brothers' research showed that trades of 100 shares or less had accounted for less than 1 percent of the volume on the NYSE for that day—the lowest level in history. The individual investor was truly getting squeezed out of the market.

This phenomenon had not gone undetected by the financial press. In a November 1984 article in the *New York Times,* Richard McCabe of Merrill Lynch, Pierce, Fenner & Smith was quoted as saying, "Investors are fearful that market rallies won't last."[9] In other words, the type of market environment created by institutional trading caused the small investor to stay on the sidelines. One week later the *Times* again tackled the subject. In an article titled "How the Institutions Rule the Market," the reporter stated, "The upshot is that the John and Jane Does of America have been bailing out of the stock market for a year and a half now, ever since the big rally

---

[8]Laszlo Birinyi, Jr., Jody E. Needle, Linda S. Rohr, Charles E. Miles, and Julie E. Morrison, *Equity Market Review and Outlook— 1984–85* (New York: Salomon Brothers, 1985).

[9]Fred R. Bleakley, "Wanted on Wall Street: Individual Investors," *New York Times,* November 18, 1984.

FIGURE 1-1 Block Volume as a Percentage of Total NYSE Volume, 1978–1984

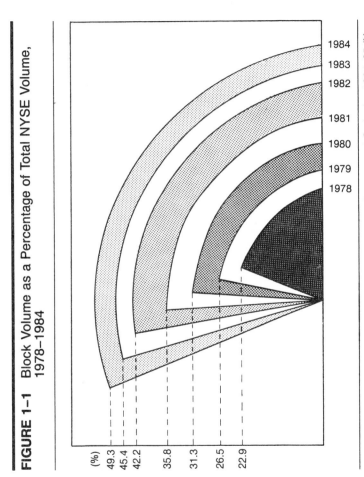

SOURCE: Laszlo Birinyi, Jr., et al., *Equity Market Review and Outlook—1984–85* (New York: Salomon Brothers, 1985).

of 1982 and 1983 ended."[10] A press release from the New York Stock Exchange in December 1985 qualified this trend. It showed that from mid-1983 to mid-1985 the number of NYSE-listed shareowners declined 3 percent.[11]

What remains is a self-fulfilling prophecy. As institutional trading increases, it creates market environments that dissuade individual investors from participating. This in turn increases the percentage of total trading represented by institutions, which drives out even more individual investors. The net result is that institutions are becoming an ever-larger factor in stock market activity. Their growing involvement will lead to a continuation of the present environment: sudden, short, sharp moves with little or no forewarning and rarely any follow-through.

THE CREEPING VOLATILITY: INTEREST RATES AND BONDS

If this new era of volatility were strictly limited to the equity markets, its damaging effects would be limited—at least to some extent. Unfortunately, this was not the case. Other sectors of the investment world began to reflect similar symptoms at the same time. As Figure 1–2 shows, during the late 1970s and early 1980s the debt markets were converted from a sleepy backwater into as boisterous a marketplace as the stock market.

The culprit in this instance was even more readily identifiable—the Federal Reserve Board. The 70s had seen drastic changes in the U.S. monetary system. We had scrapped the gold standard and trashed the Bretton

---

[10]Michael Blumstein, "How the Institutions Rule the Market," *New York Times,* November 25, 1984.

[11]"Shareownership 1985 at a Glance," New York Stock Exchange, December 4, 1985.

FIGURE 1–2 Interest Rate Volatility (quarterly change in yield of 20-year Treasuries)

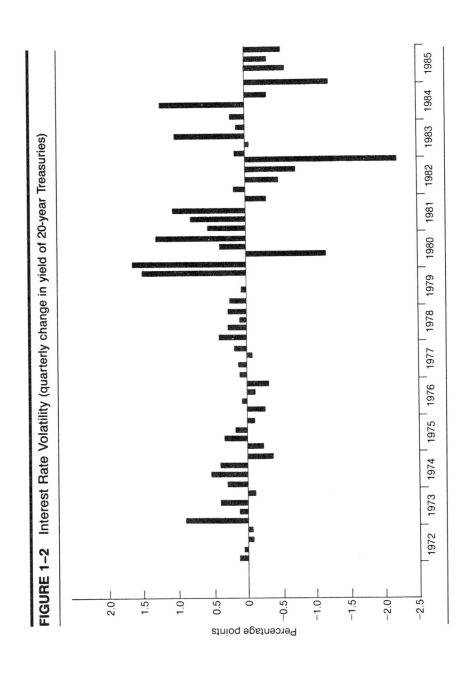

Woods foreign exchange system.[12] Finally, as a result of expansionary economic policies during the 70s, which had seen the advent of double-digit inflation, monetary policy shifted from an interest rate standard to a money supply standard. In other words, the Federal Reserve chose not to control interest rates but to control the total supply of money in the economy. Shortly after that decision was made in October 1979, its results became apparent.

Figure 1–2 shows that while interest rates were once extremely stable and fluctuated within a relatively tight band, they now gyrated wildly. One must understand the effect such gyrations would have on outstanding bonds: bonds are issued with a fixed coupon but are subsequently "marked to the market" as interest rates change. In other words, if a bond is issued with a 10 percent coupon and market interest rates move down to 5 percent, the price of that bond will move from 100 (or par) to near 200, so that its current yield will be the same as that of new bonds issued with a 5 percent coupon. In an era of stable interest rates, such as those we had prior to October 1979, there is little movement in prices. In fact, before 1979 the standard of trading was 1/64 of a point (or 15 cents per bond). By the early 80s it was not uncommon to read of 30-year Treasuries moving 2½ points (or $25) in a single day.

Going from a 15-cent standard to a $25 standard created significant disruptions. As this era began, interest rates hovered near 20 percent. This meant that dealers purchasing bonds for their own account in order to maintain an orderly market were doing so with a

---

[12] The gold standard set a predetermined amount of gold held by the U.S. government to back each dollar in circulation. Bretton Woods had established a system of fixed exchange rates between the world's major currencies.

"negative carry." (This means that the cost of financing purchases is greater than the income earned through accrued interest.) The result: dealers who might have been in a position to provide some sense of orderliness to otherwise suddenly volatile markets did not want to do so. The ultimate result bordered on chaos. Many felt that the once-staid bond markets had run amok.

VOLATILITY AND FOREIGN CURRENCY EXCHANGE

Creeping volatility has not stopped with the bond markets. The once-secure arena of foreign currency exchange has been exposed as well. Until a few short years ago the sole participants in this market were banks, multinational companies, and a handful of sophisticated traders. With few exceptions their participation in the market was for nontrading, business-related purposes: banks because of their international dealings, and corporations to cover "exposed" positions of their overseas subsidiaries. As in the bond market of old, transactions were very mundane.

This is no longer the case today, however. Once again the culprit is easily identified. It is the advent of "currency traders," which followed the development of futures and option trading in currencies. Today, currency traders—who are sometimes referred to as the "players"—can easily participate in this segment of the marketplace—and with good leverage as well. Many futures and option contracts require no more than a 1 to 2 percent cash investment as a percentage of the dollar value of the position that is carried. By way of comparison, a 50 percent margin is currently required on equity positions. The *Los Angeles Times* has recently described the once-mundane currency market in the following terms:

The currency market is as volatile as any, and regular crises make (the trader's) job among the highest-pressure, highest-risk jobs in the financial world. . . . The burden has also grown in recent years as the currency market has gotten bigger and more volatile.[13]

Because of the easygoing rules that now govern the currency market, it is not surprising that this segment of the market has had such a rapid growth. One of the major sources of data on currency trading is through the financial markets' news terminals maintained by the Reuters news agency of London. Between 1980 and 1985 the number of such terminals rose from 15,000 to 48,000, and between 1984 and 1985 the number of "dealing terminals"—that is, terminals through which trades can be executed—doubled. The *Los Angeles Times,* in the article cited above, estimated that the number of currency trading desks in New York City alone has increased by one third in the last 10 years. Overall, it was recently estimated that the daily trading volume in currency exceeds $150 billion, or approximately *40 times more than the dollar value of daily trading on the New York Stock Exchange;* the volume of currency trading often reaches $200 billion in a single day.

The result is again very similar to what has transpired in the bond market. In the past, a one-day change in value for the dollar of a fraction of a cent was considered significant. But in recent times the markets have observed 1 percent swings in a matter of hours. One-day price swings of 4 percent have already occurred. And once again, as in the case of both the stock and bond markets, these dramatic trends have developed within the past decade. This has left participants little if any time to adjust.

---

[13] Paul Richter, "Currency Trade: Risky Business," *Los Angeles Times,* October 4, 1985.

* * *

To sum matters up, volatility has struck the investment markets. Rules that worked in the old environment no longer apply. The traditional patterns have been so disrupted that one can scarcely believe they will ever return. Because of the shortened time frame and heightened dynamics of today's markets, no one should be surprised at the negative influences that have resulted. While gradual changes would allow investors sufficient time to make adjustments, the rapid changes described in this chapter have caused virtually insurmountable problems. We will look at the aftermath of the recent revolution in the marketplace in the next chapter.

How Volatility Affects Investors

For the traditional investor in stocks and bonds, the effect of volatility has been totally counterproductive. The traditional portfolio, spread across a broad cross section of issues, was designed to reduce risk while achieving the desired objectives. That was fine in a stable, slow-moving market environment, where the portfolio manager (or the individual investor) had sufficient time to control this broadly based portfolio. But in a volatile environment of short, sharp markets, the reverse occurs; in effect the portfolio controls the investor. It becomes too unwieldy a vehicle for the investor to manage effectively in a rapidly evolving market.

THE SLOWNESS OF DECISION MAKING

A look at the mechanics of decision making at the institutions that dominate the marketplace demonstrates the quandary these firms now face. Most medium-to-large investment management firms employ a team of analysts, portfolio managers, and senior investment officers to analyze developments in the economic, monetary, and political spheres, and to assess how such developments might affect the markets as a whole, individual sectors of the market, or particular securities. The inputs of this team are digested by a central investment policy committee that determines the complexion of the portfolios managed by the firm. In many cases the process of implementing those decisions can take weeks or months. One very large trust bank has openly admitted that it would take six to nine months for it to sell out its larger positions.

Let's imagine that the investment policy committee of such an organization held a regularly scheduled meeting during the first week of August 1984, that the committee correctly observed the drastic change in the market, and that it decided to take action. By the time those decisions could filter down to the individual portfolio managers who could make changes in individual client portfolios, the market rally would have ended. For example, any portfolio modifications implemented after August 7 would have served no useful purpose since the rally was virtually over by August 3. Markets today move more rapidly than most decision makers can react.

THE PROBLEM OF LIQUIDITY

As a result, we are now witnesses to a new phenomenon. Realizing that speed is of the essence, many institutions are attempting to undertake similar portfolio steps in the same compacted time frame. The problem is that the markets can only absorb efficiently so much of this type of panic buying or selling at a time. This results in the illiquidity of seemingly liquid issues. (Liquidity means the ability to trade at or near previous prices without creating disruptions.) The specialist system of trading stocks demands a basically balanced number of buyers and sellers if liquid markets are to be maintained.

Liquidity has suffered today as behemoth institutions trade voluminous amounts of stocks. This is because often all or most of these institutions wish to buy or sell at the same time. All too frequently we have seen in recent years the price of stocks such as Coleco Industries, Inc., Data General, Texas Instruments Incorporated, Warner Communications, and others with a high percentage of their outstanding shares held by institutions, plunge suddenly as much as 30 percent in value. As Steven C. Leuthold pointed out in Chapter One, specialists facing a sudden, huge influx of institutional buyers or sellers would be foolhardy to commit their own capital in an attempt to maintain an orderly market. And, as a result, we have the free-fall.

After an institutionally triggered selling panic in October 1978, *The Wall Street Journal* ran a front-page story about illiquid assets under the headline, "Stock Market Is Hurt by Woes of Investors Trying to Sell Shares." The reporter stated:

> Stock market declines as steep as the latest one sometimes carry their own antidote, washing out "weak" holders and touching off bargain buying as investors bravely gamble that the worst is over. Sometimes. This time analysts aren't so sure. . . . "It's impossible for me to get out," says one money manager caught owning a stock and looking for a chance to sell it. "I can't even sell 5,000 shares." That's obviously an exaggeration. He could sell 5,000 shares if he were willing to accept a much lower price. . . . Whatever else the latest market decline did, it clearly exposed a weak liquidity condition that could plague investors for many more weeks and until it improves, poses the threat of further "free-fall" drops in stock prices like those of late October.[1]

The reporter was accurate, except in one respect. The problem did not end in a matter of months, but continues to this very day!

TWO GROUPS AT A DISADVANTAGE

In addition, two other bastions of the traditional market have been detrimentally affected by the market's heightened volatility and illiquidity. The first is the *buy-and-hold school of thought* whose followers believe that stocks are one-decision instruments that require intensive research only at their point of purchase. Thereafter, according to this school, the stocks can be "put away in the vault" for a period of years. Of late, this thesis has been sorely tested. Even students of Graham & Dodd—the leading proponent of "basic value" investing that recom-

---

[1]Charles J. Elia, "Illiquid Assets," *The Wall Street Journal,* November 16, 1978.

mends buying solid, established companies with good balance sheets—have discovered that a "basic value" can become "overvalued" within a matter of months or days. The technique of this school may continue to work for some investors, but it requires greater agility as well as more intensive supervision on their part.

A second group of investors left at a disadvantage today includes *technicians,* or *chartists.* Its members reach buy-and-sell decisions, either on the market as a whole or on individual stocks, from a purely technical viewpoint. Again, because of today's shortened time frame and abrupt changes in the market's direction, technical analysis is often slow in its timing or misleading in its conclusions. A 30-point, one-day move in the DJIA may trigger buy signals on many trend-sensitive technical systems. But if that one-day move proves to be an aberration, as has frequently been the case in recent years, such signals may precipitate activity leading to negative results.

Consequently, the broadly diversified traditional portfolio has two glaring weaknesses today: (1) it will prove, as a whole, unwieldy to manage in a fast-paced market environment; and (2) the more diversified the portfolio, the more likely it is to contain one or more issues that will experience a sudden free-fall. Over 50 percent of a portfolio may be performing as expected, but one or two issues that become sudden plungers can make the total portfolio's performance substandard. This is the paradox faced by professional equity managers today.

The individual investor is at an even greater disadvantage. First, he or she has been squeezed out of effectively participating in the stock market by giant institutional investors. By way of analogy, let's picture someone sitting down at a "friendly" poker game with a stake of a few hundred dollars, when all the other players at the table have stakes totaling in the thousands. It will not be long before that individual is forced out of the game. Small investors in today's stock and bond marketplace face the same predicament. The game is stacked against them.

Second, individual investors lack the personnel and analytic resources of their institutional counterparts. What chance do individual investors have to correctly anticipate key market turning points, such as those of August 1982 or August 1984? What chance that they will foresee a free-fall situation in an individual position before it occurs? Since individual portfolios are generally less diversified than institutional portfolios, imagine the impact when a sudden drop hits a stock within a portfolio containing only 5 to 10 issues. Can individual investors utilizing the services of a broker, relying on tips from friends and associates, or tracking their portfolios on a part-time basis ever hope to anticipate developments? No wonder individual investors are leaving the marketplace en masse!

IMPACT ON THE BOND MARKET

Dramatic as the effect volatility has had both on individual and professional stock investors, its impact on the bond market has been even more pronounced. For all intents and purposes, prior to October 1979 there was no need for active bond management since prices barely moved in either direction. Assembling a debt portfolio in those languorous days was quite simple. An assortment of 30-year U.S. Treasuries and AAA corporate bonds were purchased and put away in the vault. Every six months interest coupons were clipped, and at maturity bonds were handed in for redemption. They rarely if ever moved in price, so why should an investor follow them on a day-to-day basis?

Since 1979 everything has changed. Balanced investors purchasing both stocks and bonds for their portfolios can no longer devote all their attention to the equity half alone; the present-day volatility in the bond market demands equal attention be paid to the debt portion of the portfolio as well. Income investors have had to develop the analytical skills of active bond management. This is particularly evident among Wall Street firms serving the institutional market. After the changes that occurred in October 1979, these firms had to secure the services of bond analysts and bond market strategists.

Equity investors (investors in stocks) can take some small comfort in the fact that even before the high volatility of the last 10 years affected the stock market, security analysis was available to assess market values on a rational basis. Such was not the case with the bond market. As bond prices began to gyrate, there was no ready pool of information on which investors could draw in order to judge whether bonds were overpriced, fairly priced, or undervalued. And thus, the disruptions in the bond market have been far more pronounced than those in the stock market.

The effect of these disruptions has been just short of devastating for professional money managers in the bond area. One observer remarked, "The greater volatility of bond returns...has seemingly thrown asset management into disarray."[2] And a leading institutional investor commented, "Bonds are unquestionably less perfect as a means of funding future pension liabilities.... There is no longer a really low-risk (investment) for long-term funding."[3] This outlook, while dismal, is quite realistic. Bonds are no longer the safe haven they once represented.

---

[2] Kimberly Blanton, "New Bond Risks Raise Mix Questions," *Pensions & Investment Age,* December 6, 1982.

[3] Ibid.

Attempts have been made to reduce the negative effects of volatility in the bond market. Such strategems include hedging with futures (buying bonds while simultaneously selling interest rate future contracts short), swaps (selling one bond and buying another with a better yield or call production), immunization (in which a pension fund will buy bonds whose maturities are in direct proportion to future funding liabilities), and convertible arbitrage (buying a convertible bond and selling short the underlying common stock, or vice versa, to "trap" a pricing discrepancy). But none of these devices has proved foolproof. The facts remain the same: For the foreseeable future, bond investors will face a market noteworthy for sharp, erratic movements that could not have been predicted a decade ago. It is difficult to visualize a return to the stability of the "good old days" in the stock market. But this is not necessarily the case in the bond market. If the Federal Reserve Board were to resume its practice of controlling interest rates, the present situation in the bond market might easily change. The Fed today uses interest rates as a device in controlling the nation's money supply. But if the Fed were to reinstate stability in interest rates, we would once again see—and within a short time—a concomitant lack of major shifts in bond prices.

* * *

Overall, the effects of volatility on the stock, currency, and bond markets have been severe. Volatility has thrown traditional methods of investment into disarray. Once-basic maxims, such as the need to maintain diversification, have been questioned and cast into disrepute. All this has occurred as a result of rapid shifts in direction of the markets along with dynamic movements never imagined only 10 years ago. As we have seen, broadly diversified portfolios have proved unwieldy and are now more of a detriment than a benefit.

Investors confronted by the problem of volatility have had to deal with still another problem—and at the same time. Like riders in a steeplechase, they have had to confront a second, seemingly insurmountable hurdle: the problem of complexity.

CHAPTER THREE

The Problem of Complexity

In this discussion complexity refers to the number and type of alternatives available to investors. The larger the list of choices, the more complex the process of creating a cohesive, well-blended portfolio becomes. To appreciate the impact complexity has had, it would once again be helpful to begin by comparing the pre-1970 environment with today's environment. The differences between then and now are striking.

THE SITUATION PRIOR TO 1970

Before 1970 most equity investments were centered in *blue chip stocks,* a small group of no more than 50 issues. These included the largest, best-established companies, such as American Telephone & Telegraph Co. (AT&T), International Business Machines Corporation (IBM), General Motors Corporation, Ford Motor Company, U.S. Steel, Bethlehem Steel, and Du Pont. Most are basic industrial companies, leaders (or second- or third-largest) within their respective industries. Because of their size, they dictate product pricing, and many are monopolistic in nature. (The Justice Department's antitrust suits against AT&T and IBM, which led to the breakup of the former, speak to this very point.) From a security analyst's point of view, the task of tracking such companies was not at all complicated. Once industry trends were assessed (particularly if the company were involved in a cyclical part of the economy), the job of coming up with valid earnings estimates and rational projections of dividend increases was rather simple. Such companies were known quantities; variability in earnings trends due to new products and potential developments was extremely low. Seasoned businesses were very predictable.

I can recall my personal experience as a "rookie" analyst in the mid-1960s, when I was told to follow a number of electric utilities. One of my senior associates quickly taught me the "tricks of the trade": I had to study the historical patterns of each company—how much its earnings rose on average each year, in *which quarter* the dividend was raised, and by how much. (Back then everyone assumed that a utility, for example, would raise its dividend each year.) I was to project the percentage increases for the coming year, and that was my estimate. To be on the safe side, an analyst also had to investigate the regulatory environment within the state or states in which that utility operated. This was to make sure that future requests for rate increases would be honored in the same expeditious manner as in the past. I found within a few quarters that as suspect as this research method might appear, it produced earnings and dividend estimates with uncanny accuracy. Such was the state of affairs in security analysis in the "good old days" prior to 1970.

The situation on the fixed income side was not much different—in other words, very limited in scope. As mentioned earlier, the bond market then consisted primarily of U.S. Treasury and Agency issues and AAA corporates. The phrase *junk bonds* had not yet been coined, particularly as it pertains to tax-exempt bonds. No fiduciary or prudent investor would consider anything other than investment-grade corporate or tax-free bonds. Besides, there wasn't much else to choose from.

Analysis? It was an unknown art at that time, except for the firms that provided ratings for debt issues. What was there to say about a 30-year U.S. Treasury bond with a 2 percent coupon that traded in daily increments of $1/64$ of a point? Or perhaps a 25-year AT&T bond with a $4\frac{1}{4}$ percent coupon that on an "active" day moved $2/32$s. What information would such an analysis have provided? That the U.S. government and AT&T were still recognizing their responsibilities pursuant to their indenture agreements to bondholders? Hardly! These bonds were items to be placed in vaults; there was no need to subject them to analysis.

TODAY'S SITUATION

By comparison, at present the spectrum of investment alternatives and the research available on them have exploded! The extent of various investment avenues has expanded from being extremely limited to seemingly boundless—all within a few short years. These investments include financial futures, emerging growth stocks, options, deep discount bonds, medical technology stocks, junk bonds, low capitalization stocks, convertibles, zeroes, high-tech/low-tech stocks, and so on, ad infinitum.

The list is lengthy and grows almost every day. Prior to the 1970s options markets did not even exist. And before 1980 there was no way to actively trade below-investment grade (or junk) bonds; the majority of such issues back then were former investment grade issues that had fallen on hard times. Original-issue junk bonds were almost unheard of. Prior to the creation of the National Association of Securities Dealers Automated Quotation system (NASDAQ), no formal marketplace (electronic or otherwise) existed for the trading of over-the-counter stocks. As a result of all these new alternatives, the dictionary of investment terminology has expanded commensurately to include such terms as *stock index futures, monoclonal antibodies* (a creation of advanced medical technology), *stripped Treasuries* (Treasury bonds from which all interest coupons have been stripped), *reorgs* (companies in bankruptcy, in the process of reorganization), *white knights* (companies that step in to prevent an unfriendly takeover), and *software* (the programs which allow computer hardware to perform various tasks). The lexicon grows progressively larger.

SIGNS OF THE TIMES

There are many signposts of the explosive growth mentioned above. A few of them are listed below:

Number of Issues Listed.   As Table 3–1 shows, the increase in the number of issues listed on the New York Stock Exchange is one aspect of the expansion.

No such precise statistics are available for over-the-counter issues, but since the debut of NASDAQ, the attractiveness of such stocks has been enhanced and expanded dramatically.

Awards to Analysts.   We can calculate the depth of coverage of the investment spectrum provided to institutions by Wall Street brokerage firms by noting the increase in number of the annual awards handed out to leading research analysts by *Institutional Investor Magazine.* In 1971—the first year of the *Institutional Investor* All-America Research Team—85 analysts were chosen in 26 industry groups. Fourteen years later, in 1985, 395 analysts were selected in 60 industry groups and other investment categories.[1]

Size of Financial Tables.   In order to gain a new perspective on the explosive growth of the financial marketplace, I examined the space occupied by financial tables in the business section of the *New York Times* at different times. The results are shown in Table 3–2.

If subtitles were listed, the true breadth of the market would be even more apparent. For instance, under Index Options are included Standard & Poor's (S&P's) options on the Chicago Board Option Exchange (CBOE); major

---

[1] Gilbert E. Kaplan, "Growth of a Feature," *Institutional Investor Magazine* (October 1985), p. 7.

TABLE 3-1 Number of Issues Listed on the New York Stock Exchange, 1960–1985

Date	Number of Issues
1/1/60	1,506
1/1/70	1,796
1/1/85	2,318

SOURCE: New York Stock Exchange Research Department. Information received by the author by telephone.

market, market value, and computer technology options on the American Stock Exchange (ASE); NYSE options on the New York exchange; gold and silver options in Philadelphia; and technology options on the Pacific exchange. Under Financial Futures Options are listed U.S. Treasury bond options on the Chicago Board of Trade (CBT) and U.S. Treasury bill options on the International Monetary Market (IMM).

The size of the business section in the Sunday edition of a major metropolitan newspaper or that of a financial publication such as *Barron's,* with its weekly summaries, has grown to such an extent that it exceeds the total size of most nonmetropolitan newspapers; and new additions are made every week or month. For instance, recently an option was created for the consumer price index (CPI); the value of the option increases or decreases commensurately with changes in the CPI. If that arrangement sets a precedent, how much longer will it be before newspapers and financial publications include a new section titled Economic Options? The fertile minds at the options and commodity exchanges might soon present us with an

TABLE 3-2 Size of Financial Tables in the *New York Times*, 1960–1985

Date	Page	Quotations	Space
January 1, 1960	1*	Over-the-counter (including mutual funds)	2 columns
	2	New York Stock Exchange	3/4 page
	3	NYSE-balance of issues—Montreal, Toronto, foreign exchanges	1/2 page
	4	Commodities, out-of-town exchanges	1 1/2 columns
	5	NYSE bonds, U.S. government and agency bonds	1/2 page
	6	American Stock Exchange (ASE)	1/2 page
January 1, 1970	1	Over-the-counter and mutual funds	Full page
	2	NYSE stocks (part 1)	Full page
	3	Out-of-town exchanges—Toronto, Montreal, foreign exchanges	3 columns +
	4	NYSE stocks (part 2)	Full page
	5	ASE stocks, NYSE stocks (part 3)	Full page
	6	NYSE stocks (balance), U.S. government and agency bonds, ASE bonds, NYSE bonds	Full page
January 1, 1985	1	NYSE stocks (part 1)	Full page
	2	NYSE stocks (part 2)	Full page
	3	ASE stocks, NASDAQ supplemental	Full page
	4	NASDAQ national market and NASDAQ national list	Full page
	5	Stock options—Chicago, Philadelphia, American, Pacific. Index options—Chicago, New York, American, Philadelphia, Pacific	Full page
	6	NYSE bonds (part 1), U.S. Treasury and over-the-counter (NASDAQ) (part 2)	Full page
	7	Financial futures, financial futures options, financial options, commodity futures, commodity options, foreign currency futures, futures	Full page
	8	NYSE bonds (part 2), government agency bonds, mutual funds, other U.S. and foreign stock exchanges	Full page

*Page shared with sports results.

auto sales option, a new housing starts index future, or a U.S. balance-of-trade option.

And if the present trend in corporate finance proceeds apace, why shouldn't there be a separate quotation table for leveraged buyouts (LBOs), mergers, and white knight instruments? Or a separate table for noninvestment grade debentures? Or two tables for mutual funds—one for equity-oriented funds, the other for fixed-income funds? As the intricacies of the financial markets multiply and create an ever-greater number of permutations and variations on themes, the total number of investment alternatives will expand accordingly.

The possibilities are limitless. Will they all come to pass? Probably not, but they do speak to the central issue. The markets are growing at a very rapid pace. New twists are emerging almost as quickly as the old ones are digested, and there is no end in sight. As with volatility, the problem of complexity is becoming more difficult instead of simpler.

How can professional or individual investors cope with such a wide spectrum of investment alternatives, particularly in today's volatile environment? Only with great difficulty, as we shall see.

CHAPTER FOUR

The Effects of Complexity

Medical technology is an area that did not even exist a few short years ago. Is one to track this exciting growth area on a part-time basis? Can an area where the state of the art is determined almost daily—where today's leading developments may be outmoded in a matter of weeks or months—be comprehended fully if we track it only a few moments per day? This is an area that obviously has potential rewards as well as commensurate risks. How many serious investors have the necessary expertise to reach the necessary judgments?

NEW INVESTMENT POSSIBILITIES

This is the task facing investors as a result of the burgeoning array of investment alternatives. We can easily summarize it: There's too much to do in too little time. With all that is involved in creating cohesive portfolios (as we shall see in Chapters Ten through Fourteen), where do we find the time to assess the risk-reward characteristics of each of these alternatives? How do we determine which, if any, of this cross section of niches belongs within our portfolio? What characteristics will the overall portfolio take on by mixing certain combinations of these alternatives? These are difficult questions to answer in any market setting. When such conclusions must be reached in a volatile environment and a much shorter time span, the task borders on the impossible. Exacerbating the problem even further is the fact that each of these niches has become so complex in itself that it requires full-time dedication just to follow any one of them. In my opinion there's no longer a stock market but rather a series of submarkets.[1]

---

[1]Statement of the author, quoted in Jaye Scholl, "Republic's Michael Hirsch Offers a Model Fund Portfolio," *Barron's,* August 15, 1983.

Let's take the example of options—an investment possibility that, like medical technology, did not exist until recently. Where does one find the time or the expertise to successfully invest in this precarious market? Virtually overnight the option area has developed such a level of sophistication that anyone approaching it on a part-time basis is left at a distinct disadvantage. Investors have to learn about buy-write programs (buying the underlying common stock and simultaneously selling an option on it), butterfly programs (a complicated series of put and call transactions), option arbitrage (capturing price differentials between different options or between options and stocks), and hedging (buying or selling puts and calls to protect a profit in a position). Should investors forsake the opportunity of including options in their portfolios because options are hard to understand? This would be unwise in view of the fact that there are a number of situations when options belong in the portfolio of a serious investor.

THE FULL SPECTRUM SCHOOL

How have professional investors reacted to this quandary? Two schools of thought have emerged. One group holds that professional money managers—whether they are bank trust officers, independent investment counselors, or financial planners—must be prepared to cover all alternatives. They must provide clients with a fullfledged investment service, encompassing the entire spectrum of investments. How can one accomplish this task? It depends on the size of the organization. The choice for the very large firm is to staff up, that is, to hire a full complement of investment specialists (analysts and portfolio managers) who can cover as many niches as possible. If the firm wants to offer its clients an options capability, it will have an options specialist on its staff. If the firm wants to offer more aggressive clients an opportunity to participate in medical technology stocks, it will hire a medical technology analyst. The full complement of specialists might number 20 or more, but at least the organization will be a full-service firm.

Two problems are apparent in this approach. First, it presumes that the firm in question will hire the best available talent in each area. If the individual hired as a convertible bond specialist turns out to be less than stellar, what next? If the firm's stock market strategist misses one too many market turns, what can be done? Few firms are capable of putting together the "ultimate" team. Second, even fewer firms have the budget to finance such a team. In this era of million dollar salaries for outstanding portfolio managers and high six-figure compensation packages for "all-star" analysts, it requires extra deep pockets to field such a team of specialists. In a 1984 article in the *American Banker,* I stated, "This is where most of those with defeatist tendencies find the 'grade up or get out' choice so perplexing. Grading up at most institutions is a financial impossibility."[2]

The choice for a small-to-medium-sized firm closely parallels that of the larger firm. But mainly as a result of the firm's size and budgetary considerations, the number of specialists hired will be far smaller. The outcome: each member of the team will have to wear more than one hat. In turn, the problems of spreading oneself too thin will begin to surface within a short time. If full-time specialists are hard-pressed to keep current with new developments, how can a team member who is forced to assume the part-time role of a specialist hope to accomplish this task?

A very small firm—I am thinking now of the prover-

---

[2]Michael D. Hirsch, "Mutual Funds: Key to Investment Management," *American Banker,* April 16, 1984.

bial one-person shop—can simply bypass the attempt to create internal research capabilities. Instead, access can be had to research via outside sources such as Wall Street analysts or independent consultants. In this case the firm's investment person will have to digest the research inputs obtained from outside sources in order to create a rational investment policy. But this choice is disappearing rapidly today, particularly because of the increasing complexity of the marketplace. Thus the sole practitioner who opts for this approach will quickly realize that by attempting to be all things to all people, he or she has become a mere jack-of-all-trades and a master of none. Small investment managers who present themselves as balanced managers must have either a large degree of self-assurance or a large capacity for self-delusion.

AN ALTERNATIVE APPROACH: THE INVESTMENT BOUTIQUE

A second school of thought holds that investment firms should not try to be all things to all clients. This group, which has surfaced in the last 5 to 10 years, has given rise to the investment boutique. This is an organization, normally small in size, that specializes in only one area of the investment spectrum. For example, a boutique known as the ABC Advisers may handle only emerging growth stocks; a second firm, the XYZ Management, may specialize in high-yielding bonds; and still a third company, DEF Investors, may deal solely in the stocks of firms in reorganization. This approach implies that because of the complexity of the market, no individual or organization can cover more than a single niche within the broad array of investment alternatives, even on a full-time basis. Each of these alternatives, it is claimed, deserves full-time attention, which is what the investment boutique delivers.

Unfortunately, there is a major problem associated with this school of thought—a difficulty affecting the clients of the investment boutique, not its owners. It may be fine to focus sharp attention on a limited portion of the investment spectrum at certain times. But to suggest that focusing on one area of specialization is always suitable would be wrong. Such an idea is not the real world! There is a time to own emerging growth stocks, but not all the time. There is a time to own deep-discount convertible bonds, but not all the time. There are tremendous investment opportunities in cyclical stocks during economic recoveries, but what about during recessions? At times it is advisable to concentrate one's focus, but not while the market's appetite is shifting so rapidly. In a word, no one has yet discovered the single investment for all seasons.

Such managers will, of course, be quick to retort, "We do not expect to be the investor's sole manager; the client should use a diversity of investment specialists, each of whom can provide expertise in a separate discipline. That way, when the firm's style of investing falls out of favor, the negative effect on the investor's total portfolio will be muted." But it is unlikely that these managers would suggest that their clients should take their business elsewhere pending "more favorable" conditions. Also, forcing clients to allocate their funds among different managers shifts two basic components of investment management— market strategy and asset allocation—from the party that has historically performed these tasks, the investment manager, to the client, who in the past has been the beneficiary of such services. How can a portfolio manager not perform portfolio management?

DRAWBACKS TO THESE TWO SCHOOLS OF THOUGHT

We must realize, therefore, that neither of these two schools of thought has been able to overcome the negative effects intrinsic to today's market, with its broad spectrum of investments. Individual investors and plan sponsors approaching this new, fast-moving, broadly diversified marketplace on their own find their task to be far more formidable. If individual investors are inclined to make their own investment judgments, they will find an overwhelming number of sources of information on each of the new market niches. But when is there sufficient time to digest and analyze all of them? The situation is the very epitome of information overload. There is simply not enough time to absorb all that is required to stay current. (As chief investment officer for a major New York City bank, I can attest to this overload; the stack of research reports received daily from Wall Street brokerage firms measures 3–6 inches.)

On the other hand, should the individual be of a mind to accept the judgment of others, confusion still reigns. The market for advisory newsletters covering each niche has proliferated as rapidly as the spectrum itself. This does not take into account such traditional sources of advice as brokerage firms, financial newspapers, and financial magazines. The confusion is heightened by the general lack of a consensus of opinion among these publications and by the inability of any one source to demonstrate consistent predictive qualities.

IN SEARCH OF A SOLUTION

What is the answer then? How do investors—individual or professional—cope with an investment environment that is becoming ever more volatile and ever more complex? Are we to see a continuation of the exodus of small investors from the marketplace? Will a majority of professional money managers continue to find it impossible to match market returns in the years ahead?

Not necessarily. The solution to all these perplexing questions is to develop a compact, liquid, and flexible investment vehicle. For these are the very traits that can overcome the problems of volatility and complexity. Fortunately, there is such a vehicle, and it has been in existence for over 60 years! It is the open-ended mutual fund.

In Part Two we will study this vehicle and see how its unique characteristics can help investors overcome both volatility and complexity. Finally, in Part Three, we will demonstrate how the unique advantages of mutual funds can be magnified by creating a broad-based portfolio of 10 to 20 funds. We will see how multifund investing is an approach for all investment objectives and all market environments.

PART TWO

The Investment Vehicle for the New Marketplace

The Origin of Mutual Funds and Their Current Explosion

What is a mutual fund? If you had asked this question of the average investor 10 to 15 years ago, you would have either received no answer at all or a feeble response at best. Frankly, not many investors then were aware of mutual funds. Today, with the growing popularity of funds as an investment vehicle, many more people can answer that question intelligently. But for those readers who have yet to study this dynamic field to any extent, here is a concise definition:

> A mutual fund is a professionally managed investment company that combines the money of many people whose goals are similar, and invests this money in a wide variety of securities. Since different investors have diverse objectives, there are a number of different kinds of mutual funds, including aggressive growth funds, money market funds, growth funds, bond funds, balanced funds, and income funds.

STRUCTURE AND TERMINOLOGY

Basically, the mutual fund is similar in structure and objective to an investment club, except that (*a*) in the case of a fund investors receive professional advice for their assets; and (*b*) a mutual fund has its own legal status, as we shall see in a moment. The facet of full-time professional management is perhaps the most critical of all those inherent to mutual funds. They offer investors *intensive, focused, full-time attention.* Later chapters will explore why this is so.

It would be helpful to review some terminology that describes the specific elements of mutual funds. Much is heard of *load* and *no-load funds.* Loads are simply funds with sales charges, the equal of a commission on a stock or bond trade. Load funds are offered through sales organizations by brokers, financial planners, and insurance agents. No-load funds are generally offered directly to the public by a mutual fund company. A recent hybrid is the *low-load fund;* in this case the mutual fund company affixes a small sales charge. Rather than re-allow, or pay out, the bulk of the sales charge to independent salespeople, as is the case with load funds, the company recaptures the full sales charge in order to pay for marketing expenses.

Net asset value is a measure of the total assets of the fund less its expenses and liabilities divided by the total number of shares currently outstanding. For example, if a fund's portfolio is worth $1,100,000, and if it has operating expenses of $100,000 and 1 million shares outstanding, then the fund's net asset value per share is $1 ($1,100,000 − $100,000 ÷ 1,000,000). For all funds the net asset value describes the price at which shares may be sold. In no-load funds it is also the price at which shares may be purchased. In load funds, shares are purchased at the *offering price,* which equals the net asset value plus the sales charge.

The *prospectus* is the fund's official document. It contains information required by the Securities and Exchange Commission (SEC), such as the fund's investment objectives, policies, services, officers, directors, methods of purchasing and redeeming shares, sales charges if any, management fees, and financial statements. Recently the SEC authorized a more streamlined prospectus; material formerly included in the bulkier format is now presented separately in a *statement of additional information* (SAI). This information is not automatically presented to a shareholder or prospect, who must specifically request it.

Two types of payments are made by most funds to their shareholders. All dividends and interest income received from the fund's underlying stock and bond positions are paid out periodically to shareholders. Net gains on the sale of underlying portfolio holdings are paid out in the form of short- and long-term capital gains distributions. Under the Internal Revenue Code funds that meet certain requirements are permitted to make such payments to their shareholders without first paying a tax on them.

FORERUNNERS OF TODAY'S FUNDS

With that description of mutual funds in mind, let us first look at the industry's roots. A number of forerunners contributed to the development of the mutual fund. They go back to the last century, specifically to the industrial boom after the Civil War. A significant portion of that expansion was financed from overseas, primarily from Great Britain, the homeland of the large investment trusts of that period.[1]

In 1873, Robert Fleming, a leading light in the investment trust arena, formed the Scottish American Investment Trust. The trust's portfolio consisted solely of bonds floated by American railroad companies. True to the practice of the day, which was to maintain the highest degree of prudence, nothing was included in this portfolio that went far beyond senior bonds in the soundest industries, such as railroads and utilities. The investment manager established a "trust" toward his investors, and they in turn put their trust in his ability to manage their investment. That sense of fiduciary responsibility severely limited the scope of potential investments, although in later years the extent of "prudent" investments would expand considerably (and even be abused harshly prior to the crash of 1929).

Other forerunners of the mutual fund surfaced in this country early in the 20th century. These included: (1)

---

[1]Hugh Bullock, *The Story of Investment Companies* (New York: Columbia University Press, 1959). Most of the citations in this chapter are taken from this work.

bank collective trusts through which a trust bank could maintain a single large investment pool of equities or bonds for its smaller trust accounts, each of which owned a pro rata share of the larger pool; (2) numerous closed-end trusts; and (3) some creatively designed quasi trusts. All these trusts had the general characteristics of the mutual fund as we know it today, including professional management and diverse investors, but none had the specific investment structure of the present-day mutual fund.

TODAY'S FUNDS

In today's terminology there are two types of mutual funds: (1) the *open-ended fund*, in which the investment company itself issues and redeems shares to and from the public every day; (2) the *closed-end fund/trust*, which issues a finite number of shares to the public only once. Any subsequent purchases or sales must be made through an over-the-counter dealer or exchange specialist.

The first true open-ended mutual fund—the Massachusetts Investors Trust—was introduced in 1924. Two more followed in the same year. But these funds were far from "barn burners." In the heady days of the roaring twenties, investors focused almost solely on closed-end trusts. Why? In a word, because of leverage. At that time most trusts leveraged their portfolios through the use of margin and other techniques. In turn, one closed-end trust would buy the shares of other trusts. As a result, an investment of $1,000 could be holding down securities worth thousands of times its value. What chance was there then for the open-ended fund in which a dollar invested got a dollar of securities, minus the fund's operating expenses?

By the end of 1929, closed-end trusts had total assets

of $2.8 billion. By comparison, the fledgling open-ended funds (all 19 of them) had accumulated a miserly $140 million. But the crash of 1929 marked a turning point. For as strongly as leverage works in the investor's favor in a rising market, it has exactly the opposite effect in a declining market (to say nothing of what transpires in a plunging market). The crash of 1929 virtually wiped out closed-end trusts as an industry, taking along with them thousands of hopeless investors. The true ascendancy of open-ended funds began a few years later in 1932. As one observer put it, "There is no historical background of serious troubles (for open-ended funds) as a result of the (1929) panic."[2]

But the ascendancy was quite muted. Little new investment capital was being generated during the depression years of the 30s. In addition, the experience with closed-end funds (let alone the scandals of the disreputable "pyramids" that were uncovered) engendered a sense of fear within the investing public that the fledgling open-ended industry was hard put to overcome. That same sense of scandal and fraud led to the inclusion of a clause in a 1936 piece of legislation—the Public Utility Holding Company Act—directing the SEC to study the investment company industry.

THE INVESTMENT COMPANY ACT OF 1940

When that study was completed in 1940, the true turning point for the mutual fund industry occurred with the enactment of the Investment Company Act. While few industry participants would have called this a turning point—it seemed to be far too harsh and restrictive a piece

---

[2] Ibid.

of legislation—this Act was the confidence builder the public desperately needed to rebuild its faith in investment companies. The safeguards in this Act provided investors with assurances that the excesses and abuses associated with the closed-end funds of the 1920s would not recur.

It would take a book to explore all of the features of the Investment Company Act, but a few of its important safeguards should be highlighted. In essence, the Act prevents any form of self-dealing and other conflicts of interest. Each fund must have an investment adviser, an independent board of directors, and an independent transfer agent and custodian. Since each mutual fund must register with the SEC before making its shares available to the public, staff members of the SEC can thoroughly check to see that a true arm's-length relationship exists among these various functionaries prior to the fund's going public. In addition, most states have enacted mutual fund regulations of their own to protect investors against self-dealing and conflicts among people offering funds to the public.

The 1940 Investment Company Act, which regulates a major component of the financial service industry, has proved to be the most restrictive in the financial area. According to Ray Garrett, Jr., former chairman of the Securities and Exchange Commission, "No issuer of securities is subject to more detailed regulation than mutual funds."[3] In fact, when questioned about what insurance is available for mutual fund investors, most fund managers will answer, "The 1940 Investment Company Act!" The fact is that no fraud of any consequence has befallen mutual fund investors since that legislation was enacted. No mutual fund shareholder has lost all or part

---

[3]Quoted in *1985 Mutual Fund Handbook* (Washington, D.C.: Investment Company Institute, 1985), p. 53.

of his or her investment for reasons other than market action. While the Act cannot guarantee profits, it protects against fraud, malfeasance, conflicts of interest, and the like.

DEVELOPMENTS BETWEEN 1945 AND 1970

Because of the confidence instilled by the Act, the gates were now wide open. As a result of the economic boom of the postwar period, people had disposable income available for investment as well as a safe avenue through which to invest those sums—mutual funds. As Table 5-1 indicates, the two and a half decades between 1945 and 1970 witnessed a dramatic increase in (a) the number of mutual funds available to the public; (b) the number of mutual fund investors; and (c) the total assets investors placed in funds. The mutual fund industry had come of age—and the best was yet to come!

THE POPULARITY CRAZE SINCE 1970

Dramatic as the 1945–70 period proved to be, the current popularity of mutual funds among both individual and institutional investors can only be described as a craze or a buying panic. Newspapers, consumer magazines, and financial publications are filled with mutual fund stories. The current rush into funds has lasted for over five years. As Table 5-1 notes, as recently as 1955 the total size of the fund industry was $7.8 billion in assets. But in 1986 the *monthly* net sales (purchases less redemptions) exceeded $12 billion for many months. Monthly sales were greater than the entire size of the industry 30 years earlier! In fact, in approximately four years the dollar value of the entire industry has quadrupled.

A good deal of this popularity can be attributed to the

TABLE 5-1   Shareholder Accounts and Total Net Assets, 1940–1970 (assets in 000s of dollars)*

Calendar Year End	Number of Companies	Number of Accounts	Assets
1940	68	296,056	$ 447,959
1941	68	293,251	401,611
1942	68	312,609	486,850
1943	68	341,435	653,653
1944	68	421,675	882,191
1945	73	497,875	1,284,185
1946	74	580,221	1,311,108
1947	80	672,543	1,409,165
1948	87	722,118	1,505,762
1949	91	842,198	1,973,547
1950	98	938,651	2,530,563
1951	103	1,110,432	3,129,629
1952	110	1,359,000	3,931,407
1953	110	1,537,250	4,146,061
1954	115	1,703,846	6,109,390
1955	125	2,085,325	7,837,524
1956	135	2,580,049	9,046,431
1957	143	3,110,392	8,714,143
1958	151	3,630,096	13,242,388
1959	155	4,276,077	15,817,962
1960	161	4,897,600	17,025,684
1961	170	5,319,201	22,788,812
1962	169	5,910,455	21,270,735
1963	165	6,151,935	25,214,436
1964	160	6,301,908	29,116,254
1965	170	6,709,343	35,220,243
1966	182	7,701,656	34,829,353
1967	204	7,904,132	44,701,302
1968	240	9,080,168	52,677,188
1969	269	10,166,788	48,290,733
1970	361	10,690,312	47,618,100

*Figures for shareholder accounts represent combined totals for Investment Company Institute member mutual fund companies. Duplications of a single individual having multiple accounts have not been eliminated.

factors mentioned earlier. Namely, there was a growing sense of futility among many investors over their inability to select individual securities in a volatile, complex marketplace. Also, fund popularity was strengthened by the favorable "taste" left with many investors by their experience with money market funds. Through such funds small investors are able to have access to the big leagues of investing, and the cash management functions are simplified, even for professional and institutional investors. For individuals, there is obviously the belief that—as the old saying goes—if you can't beat them, join them (mutual funds being one class of those institutional investors that now dominate the marketplace). Finally, as we shall see in Chapters Six and Seven, there are a number of other compelling arguments in favor of mutual funds in the new marketplace.

Because of this explosive growth, the industry has changed. No longer is it predominately "motherhood" funds, that is, portfolios composed of droll, one-decision stocks of the type that comprise major market indexes. For those who were first exposed to mutual funds during the 1950s and 60s, a second introduction to the industry today will be truly startling; it bears no resemblance to what it was a few short years ago. Today mutual funds have fresh management, better portfolio managers, and a wider range of choices. There is now a fund for every purpose.

Overall, two considerable forces have dramatically altered the shape of the industry. People's perceptions of the mutual fund industry have gone through a significant evolution, while at the same time the industry itself has mapped a new course for itself. This trend marks an industry that realizes the limited position it had as recently as 10 years ago, and appreciates the broader role it can fulfill within the current investment sphere.

Where does all that leave the mutual fund industry

today? According to the Investment Company Institute (ICI), the trade association for the fund industry, as of the end of December 1985 there were 1,071 non–money market funds (up 251 from one year prior) with total assets of *$251.6 billion*—an explosive increase of 83.5 percent in 12 months' time! Exemplifying the new broad scope of mutual fund offerings, the ICI classified these funds in the following categories (listed in the descending order of risk):

- Aggressive growth funds.
- Growth funds.
- Growth and income funds.
- Precious metals funds.
- International funds.
- Balanced funds.
- Income funds.
- Option/income funds.
- Government bond funds.
- GNMA funds (Government National Mortgage Association obligations).
- Corporate bond funds.
- Municipal bond funds (excluding limited term).
- State municipal bond funds.

For those interested in short-term cash equivalent investments there were also limited-term municipal bond funds and money market funds, for a grand total of 1,531 funds.

Figure 5–1, which traces the growth of the industry between 1940 and 1984, shows a most impressive growth in the number of funds after 1970.

Even more exciting has been the growth in the dollar value of the funds since 1970, as indicated in Table 5–2. Three consecutive years of net sales exceeding $25 billion in each year have thrust the industry into previously uncharted territory. During the three years ending December 31, 1985, alone, the sales of non–money market

FIGURE 5-1   Number of Mutual Funds, 1940–1984

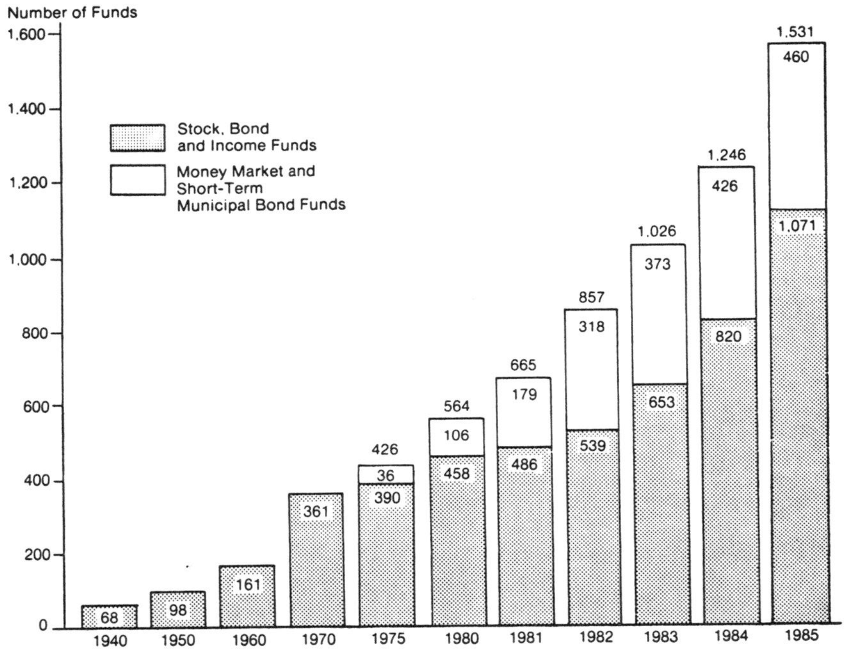

SOURCE: *Mutual Fund Fact Book • 1985* (Washington, D.C.: Investment Company Institute, 1985), p. 23.

funds topped *$200 billion*. This figure exceeded the sales of the preceding 17 years combined.

Finally, we should examine this growth from the perspective of the new and diverse types of funds that have become available in recent years.

Some interesting trends become apparent from studying Table 5–3. First of all, there was very little growth in the industry during the first half of the 70s. Obviously, this was a direct result of the steep slide in the stock market during 1973–74. In fact, between 1970 and 1975

TABLE 5-2   Sales, Redemptions, and Assets; Equity, Bond, and Income Funds (billions of dollars)

Year	Sales	Redemptions	Net Sales	Assets
1971	$ 5.1	$ 4.8	$ 0.3	$ 55.0
1972	4.9	6.6	(1.7)	59.8
1973	4.4	5.7	(1.3)	46.5
1974	3.1	3.4	(0.3)	34.1
1975	3.3	3.7	(0.4)	42.2
1976	4.4	6.8	(2.4)	47.6
1977	6.4	6.0	0.4	45.0
1978	6.7	7.2	(0.5)	45.0
1979	6.8	8.0	(1.2)	49.0
1980	10.0	8.2	1.8	58.4
1981	9.7	7.5	2.2	55.2
1982	15.7	7.6	8.1	76.8
1983	40.3	14.7	25.6	113.6
1984	45.9	20.0	25.9	137.1
1985	114.3	33.8	80.6	251.7

SOURCE: *Mutual Fund Fact Book • 1985* (Washington, D.C.: Investment Company Institute, 1985), p. 25.

net assets of aggressive growth funds, growth funds, growth and income funds, and balanced funds *declined.* The mutual fund industry, dominated as it was at that point by equity funds, could not withstand the sharp decline in the stock market. In reality, then, the dramatic growth within the industry has occurred over the last decade alone. Only in the latter half of the 70s did industry leaders discover that there was a market for other than equity funds. In fact, it was the public's overwhelmingly strong reaction to money market funds that led to this discovery. Because of the broad array of funds available today, it would take a total collapse of the capital market to have a mutual fund industry with significantly declining net assets under management.

TABLE 5–3   Growth of Mutual Funds, 1970–1985

Types of Funds	1970	1975	1980	1985
Aggressive growth funds	58	56	53	141
Growth funds	144	145	137	215
Growth and income funds	92	85	77	151
Precious metals funds	NA	NA	NA	17
International funds	NA	NA	NA	38
Balanced funds	29	28	21	24
Income funds	38	41	56	82
Option/income funds	NA	NA	10	17
Government bond funds	NA	NA	NA	53
GNMA funds (Government National Mortgage Association obligations)	NA	NA	NA	34
Corporate bond funds	NA	35	62	124
Municipal bond funds	NA	NA	42	101
State municipal bond funds	NA	NA	NA	74
Total	361	390	458	1,071

SOURCE: Investment Company Institute—Research Department.

The sales record between 1983 and 1985 bears out this opinion. In 1983 both the stock and bond markets were still looked upon favorably by investors. Of the $25.6 billion in net sales that year, $13.2 billion were in equity funds while $12.4 billion were in bond and income funds. The following year was a different story. With the stock market languishing, mutual fund net sales were still high ($25.8 billion), but only $7.7 billion came from equity funds, while the newly favored bond and income area generated $18.1 billion. In 1985 the attractiveness of bond and income funds continued, particularly because of sharply lower short-term rates ($71.1 billion). Since the stock market was on the rebound that year, equity fund sales increased as well to $9.5 billion. This epitomizes the scope of the industry at present.

PRESENT–DAY IMPORTANCE OF THE INDUSTRY

What also is important to note is the new-found importance of the industry. Over the last decade alone, the number of funds available to the public has almost tripled. Lastly—and this point is probably of utmost importance for professionals considering using mutual funds in client portfolios but fearing clients' aversion to funds—the industry's acceptance by the investing public has continued to expand dramatically. As we saw in Table 5–1, the number of shareholder accounts in all mutual funds increased to more than 10 million by 1970 (this total actually declined over the next five years to 9.7 million). Over the 10 years from 1975 to 1985, this number tripled to over 30 million! As Figure 5–2 shows, the mutual fund has clearly become an integral part of the public's preferred investment avenues.

So pronounced is this trend that the stock exchanges have had to admit to its growing importance. The *New York Times* reported in December 1985:

> The number of individuals who invest in the stock market has risen 11 percent over the last two years, but the increase has come from individuals buying through mutual funds rather than trusting their own stock-picking abilities, according to a survey that the New York Stock Exchange released today at the annual meeting of the Securities Industry Association.[4]

Nor has this acceptance been limited to the small, unsophisticated investor, the historical target of mutual fund marketing efforts. Professionals have joined in as well. By the end of 1984, 38 percent of mutual fund assets were held by institutional investors, excluding IRA and

---

[4] James Sterngold, "Investor Rise Tied to Mutual Funds," *New York Times*, December 5, 1985.

FIGURE 5–2 Assets and Shareholder Accounts for All Types of Funds (year end)

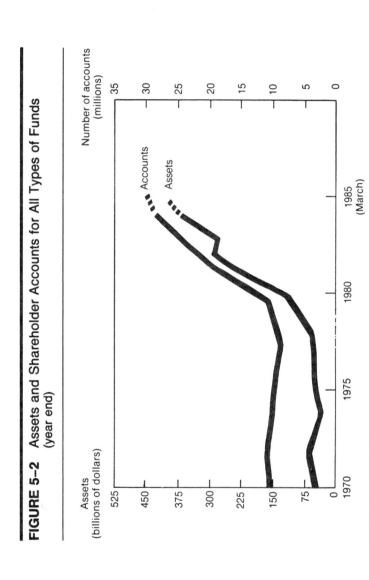

SOURCE: *Mutual Fund Fact Book • 1985* (Washington, D.C.: Investment Company Institute, 1985), p. 23.

TABLE 5-4	Institutional Mutual Fund Holdings

Year	Amount
1970	$ 6.2 billion
1974	7.1 billion
1980	17.7 billion
1983	26.0 billion
1984	140.0 billion

SOURCE: Investment Company Institute—Research Department.

Keogh accounts. Approximately 1 out of 10 shareholder accounts was owned by an institution. While the $140 billion of institutional assets in mutual funds by the end of 1984 were primarily in money market funds ($105 billion), a not inconsequential $35 billion were invested in stock and bond funds. As Table 5–4 indicates, the commitment of professional investors to the mutual fund marketplace has expanded in recent years about as much as the commitment of individual investors.

A number of events have facilitated the growing use of mutual funds by all types of institutions. First, in September 1976, the office of the Comptroller of the Currency issued revised Trust Banking Circular No. 4, which authorized trust banks to invest fiduciary assets in mutual funds provided such authority was permitted by state statutes and the trust's governing instrument. Although it was not specifically stated, the Comptroller seemingly believed that the benefits provided by mutual funds outweighed any potential liability from incurring extra investment costs or abrogating investment responsibility to a third party. Second, in October 1976 the Investment Work Group of an advisory council formed by the U.S. Department of Labor concluded a study into the investment of retirement plan assets governed by the Employee Retirement Income Security Act of 1974 (ERISA). The group reported:

> The purchase of. . . mutual fund shares. . . may provide benefits similar to naming qualified professional investment managers and may be particularly beneficial for smaller plans in meeting the prudence and diversification standards of ERISA.[5]

These two primary institutional markets—trust banks and retirement plans—were now in a position to make substantial use of mutual funds in their portfolios. As the statistics in Table 5–4 reflect, this is exactly what transpired.

* * *

As we enter the second half of the 80s, the idea of mutual funds as a legitimate investment vehicle for all types of investors has obviously taken hold of the public's imagination. Let us now examine the particular features of the funds that uniquely qualify them to fulfill investors' expectations in a volatile, complex environment.

---

[5]Report of the Investment Work Group of the ERISA Advisory Council of the U.S. Department of Labor, October 13, 1976.

The Solution to the Problems of Volatility and Complexity

As we saw in Chapters One and Two, the investment markets today are marked by sharp turns in direction and by market movements—or by segments of a cycle—of short duration. This places the traditional portfolio, broadly diversified across a wide cross section of stocks and/or bonds, at a distinct disadvantage. Such portfolios simply cannot be restructured quickly enough to reflect the rapid changes in market sentiment. As a pundit once quipped, "It would be like trying to turn a supertanker around in the middle of the ocean."

HOW TO CREATE A COMPACT, MANAGEABLE PORTFOLIO

It would be imprudent to sacrifice the safety provided by diversification in an attempt to cope with a volatile state of affairs. Just the opposite is true—the more volatile the market, the greater is the need for risk-aversion. The question, then, is quite basic: Is it possible to create a compact, manageable portfolio without sacrificing diversification? The answer is an unqualified yes! You can do so through mutual funds.

If you own a single share of a mutual fund, you automatically own a representative portion of a broadly diversified portfolio (the underlying stock/bond portfolio of that fund). And yet, since your means of ownership is that single share, you have the compactness necessary to cope with volatility. But even that compactness is not in itself the answer. For in addition to compactness, investors also need liquidity.

By liquidity we mean those financial assets that can be readily converted into cash or other forms of financial assets. By comparison, a unit in a real estate limited partnership is compact since a unit holder has a pro-rata share in a property or group of properties. But such an asset is not liquid. There is no available means of quickly converting that ownership position into cash. Compactness, therefore, is only half the answer to volatility; the key is liquidity.

In terms of stock and bond investing, *there is no more liquid means of participation than mutual funds.* They are the very epitome of liquidity. For years it was believed that stocks listed on national exchanges provided all the liquidity one would normally require. A specialist managing the order book on the floor of the exchange was assigned to each issue and empowered to maintain "orderly" markets. Theoretically, if a buyer were willing to pay the offering price, or a seller were willing to accept the bid price, the specialist would supply the necessary liquidity by selling short the shares to the buyer if insufficient shares for sale were available. Or that same specialist would buy the shares from the seller for his own account if enough buyers were not available.

But as market specialist Stephen C. Leuthold correctly pointed out in Chapter One, in this day of institution-dominated markets when buyers and sellers are dealing in tens and hundreds of thousands of shares, no specialists in their right minds would commit their own capital to provide liquidity and maintain an orderly market. Instead, what we have of late are stampedes, with all the concomitant panic. If you are the holder of 50,000 to 100,000 shares of a suddenly out-of-favor stock, and if you know that there are dozens of your peers in a similar position, prudence has of late come to mean, "Get me out at any price." This leads to an order imbalance, which remains until the specialist is able to determine how low price levels must drop for buyers to be found in order to satisfy the rampaging herd's desire to get out at any price. Only in a manner of speaking, then, are stocks still liquid if you are satisfied with receiving up to one third less for your shares than they were worth but one day earlier.

Mutual funds, on the other hand, provide true liquidity. And here again, we can look to the Investment Company Act of 1940 for the reason. According to a provision of that Act, all open-ended mutual funds must honor all buy-and-sell orders on the day they are received. The fund itself becomes the other side of the trade. If you wish to buy shares, the fund simply issues new shares. If you are a seller, the fund merely redeems those shares. More important, all this occurs with absolutely no impact on price! Remember, the mutual fund is a large elastic pool of capital, representing the combined assets of many investors. If at the close of business on a given day, the fund has net assets of $100,000, and there are 1,000 shares outstanding at that point, the net asset value per share is $100. If a new investor comes along and wishes to invest $1,000 in the pool, the fund issues 10 new shares at $100 per share. The fund now has net assets of $101,000 and 1,010 shares outstanding. (The reverse occurs when you wish to sell out of a fund position.)

Thus there is no fear of getting caught in a sudden stampede, or of attempting to sell shares on the floor of the exchange and receiving the report "stock ahead." In addition, you will not witness rapid shifts in price strictly because of buying or selling pressures, not because of fundamental reasons. Theoretically, if the vast majority of a fund's shareholders sought to liquidate on a single day, the management company would find itself in a bind because it would be forced to sell off an appreciable portion of its underlying portfolio quickly in order to raise sufficient cash. Yet since 1940 this problem has never occurred—probably because a typical fund's list of shareholders is such a diverse group of individuals and institutions. But if that problem were to occur, the fund shareholder would receive at the worst a pro-rata portion of the fund's underlying securities in lieu of cash. Short of this exceptional case, the serious investor knows, therefore, that through mutual funds he or she can move as rapidly as the market itself.

TELEPHONE EXCHANGE PRIVILEGES

Since a sufficient number of mutual funds are currently available that provide telephone exchange privileges (whereby investors can switch from one fund to another fund within the same mutual fund complex by placing a phone call), there is nothing hindering investors from altering the complexion of their portfolios with no more than one or two telephone calls. For instance, let us say that an investor has grown wary of the stock market's prospects. Through the traditional approach, changing his or her portfolio composition would require the sale of perhaps 10 or 20 security positions. When proceeds from those sales became available, the investor would have to purchase an equal dollar amount of bonds or short-term money market investments. With mutual funds, however, the investor can use exchange privileges to accomplish the same result by placing a telephone call to the fund's shareholder service number and by instructing them to transfer a certain dollar amount or an entire position in a growth or aggressive growth fund into that group's bond fund or money market fund.

In most cases the cost of this transaction will be no more than a nominal service charge (about $5). Besides the convenience afforded, the cost savings for an active investor are significant. There is no chain of commissions on 10 to 20 sell orders nor a series of commissions to buy the replacement positions.

LETTERS OF INSTRUCTION

If the individual is considering an investment in a fund that is not part of a family of funds, or in a group that does not provide telephone exchange privileges, all that would be required to achieve the same effect would be a properly prepared letter of instruction to the fund's transfer agent. "Market timers," people who invest in three or four funds at a time, have letters of instruction to liquidate readied and properly certified on the day following purchases. When the signals tell them that it is time to get out of the market, they dash off to the post office or one of the express letter services to execute their changes. According to this scenario, total portfolio modification can be accomplished by Decision Day plus one. In either case, by using the telephone or express mail, investment decisions implemented through mutual funds can be quickly modified or totally altered.

THE LIQUIDITY FACTOR

Liquidity is the antidote to volatility, and liquidity is exactly what mutual funds provide. At the same time, there is no sacrifice in diversification associated with the compactness of funds. On the contrary, the typical mutual fund portfolio is much more diversified than the typical individual or professional investor's portfolio. So the safeguards of diversification are retained, while the benefits of compactness and liquidity are gained. There is, thereby, a certain efficiency to mutual funds that lends itself perfectly to the current volatility in the investment world. Multifund investing carries this notion a step further.

Let me give you here an example drawn from my own experience. I am currently managing approximately 200 client portfolios with a wide range of investment objectives. A typical portfolio is invested in 10 to 20 mutual funds. When our firm's Investment Policy Committee decides to alter our investment philosophy, those changes will be reflected in all our clients' portfolios within 24 hours.

Since mutual funds provide both diversification and compactness, we can take advantage of this efficiency and create "superdiversification" by constructing a portfolio of funds rather than by investing in only one or two funds. We will analyze this concept in Part Three.

IN-DEPTH COVERAGE OF THE ENTIRE SPECTRUM OF INVESTMENTS

Mutual funds are equally noteworthy in their ability to overcome the difficulties created by complexity. As detailed in Chapter Three, the scope of investment alternatives has exploded in a little over 10 years' time. Formerly we had to deal only with a handful of stocks and bonds, which were rather simple, straightforward investments. By contrast, we are overwhelmed today by numerous disciplines, each of which has developed an intricacy of its own. The result is a stock and bond market that, in reality, is now a series of submarkets. In Chapter Four we explored the different ways in which institutions and individuals are attempting to cope with this expansion. Neither the full spectrum school nor the investment boutique has proved completely successful.

But mutual funds allow us to cope with the present-day marketplace because from among the over 1,300 non-money market funds currently available, we can find in-depth coverage of the entire spectrum of investments. In addition, the coverage is provided on a most timely basis. Let a new "discipline" surface, and within a short time there will emerge at least one fund through which the investor can have access via professional management to that particular area. For instance, shortly after the development of sophisticated, covered option-writing programs, the market was presented with the first of many option income funds. The first medical technology fund came out of registration in 1979. At that time many investors were not yet conversant with this emerging area, but there are now over half a dozen such funds.

An institution—whatever its size and whatever its budget for staff—need no longer wonder how to provide broad-based coverage. All the coverage it needs can come through the new, expanded world of mutual funds. An institution's research staff now resides off premises; it is a 1,300-member "farm team," standing by at the ready to allow the fiduciary to access whichever segments of the market spectrum are deemed prudent for a specific client or group of clients. In addition, as we saw in the last chapter, this access is available through a most efficient conduit: the open-ended fund. If the concept is adopted to the extent I shall propose in Part Three of this book—Multifund Investing—there will be no need at all for a research team. For example, the investment department of my own institution does not have a single analyst on its staff.

Obviously, the same premise holds true for individual investors as well. Yes, there are individuals who continue to feel capable of selecting individual securities, some via brokerage house research reports, others via intensive reading of financial journals, yet others by tips and recommendations from friends and associates. But for those who are not comfortable with such methods, the necessary answer is mutual funds. Whatever your objectives, whatever your ability to absorb risk, there is a mutual fund to fit the bill. And because of the efficiency of the funds, however hectic your lifestyle may be, a full range of investment alternatives can be built into an investment portfolio at a minimum of effort. No need to spend hour after hour of your time poring over publications and research reports and then relying on someone else's judgment. (It is only fair to point out that the authors of such articles and reports have much less at stake than the managers of mutual funds.) Instead, your total investment needs can now be accomplished through a compact portfolio of funds.

There are a number of additional considerations worthy of attention. One is the quality of the advice being offered. Let us assume that an institution has focused on deep discount bonds as an investment area it believes it must make available to its clients. As we pointed out in Chapter Four, a search would be conducted to find a qualified analyst or portfolio manager with an established reputation in this discipline. Obviously, this person's recognized talents and expertise will dictate his or her salary level. Conversely, whatever that firm's salary limitations for a single analyst or portfolio manager will dictate the level of the "quality" advice it can provide to its clients.

On the other hand, compare this state of affairs to that faced by an institution or individual that has decided to use mutual funds in lieu of analysts or portfolio managers. Here, as well, a search must be conducted, and we shall explore this process in Part Three. Assuming the search identifies a suitable "candidate"—in this case, a fund—the hiring process entails no more than a purchase order. What can you do if the candidate should later prove unsuitable? A phone call or sell order will end the relationship. From a dollars-and-cents point of view investment talent can now be added to your staff without expanding the salary budget, without incurring such items as a benefits package, travel and entertainment costs, office and telephone expenses, or the need for a support staff. By contrast, funds are a ready-made staff, and they do not involve fixed overhead expenses.

Institutional and individual investors, therefore, have at their beck and call a fully staffed team of specialists who are prepared to provide in-depth coverage of the complete spectrum of investments. This team is put together by simply placing phone calls or purchase orders.

It involves no fixed expense except for the period of time it is being used; each fund has its own built-in expense ratio. The team can be upgraded, expanded, or shrunk again and again merely as the result of a telephone call or sale order.

The fact that mutual fund investors have no fixed expenses except during the period they invest is something that merits further consideration. For this aspect clearly differentiates the traditional approach from the mutual fund approach. Let us assume that an institution has hired an analyst to cover high-tech stocks, and that later on the investment policy committee feels it is imprudent to have any high-tech exposure in client portfolios. That institution is now faced with the following questions: (1) What is the cost of liquidating all current high-tech positions in the portfolios? and (2) What can the firm do with its high-tech specialist during the time the committee decides to stay out of high-tech stocks? Such analysts are not blue-collar workers who can be temporarily laid off during a work slowdown! One does not let highly paid professionals sit around with their hands folded in their lap. Instead, what is much more likely to happen is that stocks from each niche covered by the firm's analysts will find their way into that firm's clients' portfolios. This is because exposures to niches are often cut back, but rarely liquidated completely. It is fairly easy to explain to a client why a certain position has been reduced instead of liquidated; it is far more difficult to rationalize the existence of an idle staff. The ultimate detriment is to the client.

This problem does not arise with mutual funds. Ridding one's portfolio of a suddenly undesirable investment discipline involves no personality conflicts, no idle staff considerations; it involves no more than the sale of a single fund holding or a few funds. There is no pressure because of a fixed overhead because there is no overhead at all! The cost of acquiring mutual fund talent is fixed only for the time during which an investment is made. Most funds maintain expense ratios hovering around 1 percent; by law they are capped at 1.5 percent. In other words one can have a $1 million portfolio managed for no more than $10,000 per year. This is obviously much less than the costs associated with placing a qualified analyst or portfolio manager on staff on a permanent basis.

* * *

At this point let us sum up briefly why mutual funds are such unique instruments for an investment world in a state of constant and rapid flux:

1. They offer complete, in-depth coverage of the full spectrum of investment possibilities.
2. Funds are a compact, liquid, and efficient investment vehicle.
3. There is no fixed overhead cost to investors, except for the period of time during which the investment is in place.
4. The mutual fund universe provides an adequate, easily accessible list of substitute candidates.
5. As various disciplines and market segments gain or lose favor, mutual funds offer a total ease of entry and exit for investors.

Next, in Chapter Seven, we shall take up other advantages to mutual funds.

Other Benefits of Mutual Funds

The advantages of mutual funds cited in the prior chapter are a strong reason to consider the funds for your portfolio. But there are a number of other benefits that might make the funds even more attractive, depending on the particular situation of a given individual investor or institution.

DOCUMENTED, LONG–TERM RESULTS

There are still, unfortunately, no rules governing the reporting of results by private investment managers. When an adviser shows you a statement of his or her past performance, you have no way to know whether the statement covers all accounts, a model account, or specially chosen accounts. Is it a composite return? Does it include clients who might have closed their accounts in the interim? Does it blend all types of client accounts together, including individual, corporate, and tax-exempt accounts? Does it reflect a particular client objective or link a variety of objectives? In fact, an industry panel has recently been formed to study how the reporting of investment results might be standardized.

Fortunately, this situation is not true of mutual funds, thanks to the Investment Company Act of 1940. Since open-ended funds must be prepared to issue and redeem shares daily, by definition they must also compute a net asset value (NAV) every day. The NAV is an irrefutable public record of the fund manager's performance history.

In view of the growing attention paid to funds, it is not surprising that a number of statistical services are now available to investors, including Lipper Analytical Services, CDA Investment Technologies, and Weisenberger Investment Services. These services take the daily data and create long-term performance records for the interested investor to study. Generally, the data are for various time periods and classify the funds according to their investment objectives. So readers know that they are reviewing information most pertinent to their particular situation. If you are interested in high current income, you can examine the long-term and short-term performance records of funds to see whether they are classified as seeking income or primarily fixed-income issues. No need to fear that some aggressive growth accounts have been blended in to "soup up" a fund's performance. With mutual funds, what you see is what you get!

There is one caveat, however. While a fund's long-term results are fully documented, there is always the danger that such results may be attributable primarily to a particular portfolio manager no longer in the employ of the fund.

A CONSISTENT INVESTMENT PHILOSOPHY

When an individual, plan sponsor, or other fiduciary hires a private investment counselor, such as a bank trust department or an independent investment adviser, there is a general understanding as to how that counselor will invest the client's assets. The type of security may be small growth stocks, high-grade bonds, basic industry stocks, or some combination of specific securities. Alternatively, the investment goal to be sought may be current income, long-term growth, or some combination of the two. However, there is no way to guarantee that these assumptions will be carried out. If the adviser suddenly believes that the desired objective could best be achieved by investing in another type of security, or if the portfolio manager feels that another objective is more prudent in light of prognostications about the future investment environment, the client may well end up with a portfolio quite unlike the one "contracted for."

But this is not so with mutual funds. In its prospectus, each fund must clearly state its investment objective. While there are some shortcomings in the clarity of prospectus language, as we shall later see, the fund, according to the Investment Company Act of 1940, must adhere to the guidelines outlined in the prospectus. An investor placing money in a mutual fund with a stated objective of high current income through a portfolio primarily invested in fixed-income instruments need not fear that a subsequent quarterly or semiannual fund report will reveal the portfolio to be heavily concentrated in small, over-the-counter issues. An individual or institution purchasing shares in a "government securities" fund can rest assured (assuming the prospectus so provides) that a subsequent report will not show a portfolio predominately invested in below-investment-grade corporate issues. Nothing is foolproof, but the fact is that as a result of the series of checks and balances built into the mutual fund operating structure by the Investment Company Act, not a single case of a misinvested fund has developed since 1940. Another aspect of getting what you pay for!

FULL-TIME PROFESSIONAL MANAGEMENT

One of the root causes for the inability of the traditional stock and bond approach to succeed in the present market environment has been the lack of full-time professional management. In fact, studies of investment advisory firms have shown that the individuals responsible for managing the portfolios of clients may spend up to 40 percent of their time on the solicitation and servicing of clients. In other words, such individuals are concerned with marketing, not managing. In view of the pace of today's market, is it any wonder that investment returns suffer because of so much misused time?

The mutual fund manager, by comparison, fully enjoys the benefits of an "ivory tower." Few, if any, fund managers are made available for marketing purposes. The typical fund's main marketing tools are sales materials, the prospectus, and (in the case of load funds) a sales force dealing directly with the public. In fact, perhaps the opposite is true—in many cases the fund manager is so well insulated from public exposure that we often do not know his or her identity when we invest in a fund. This is a key hurdle one must overcome in order to develop a clear picture of a fund.

What about client servicing? When you make an investment in a fund and want to speak to the "portfolio manager," the same situation exists. In most fund groups a call made to the individual managing the fund will be shunted aside to a shareholder-servicing representative. This, too, may present difficulties for the serious investor, but there are ways to overcome this situation, which we will discuss in Part Three.

Mutual fund portfolio managers who are insulated from client solicitation and retention are in an ideal position to devote their full talents to their main purpose—managing portfolios, not marketing. So when we say that the funds provide full-time management, this is truly the case. This might also help explain why, in organizations that provide both private account management and open-ended mutual funds, the funds most often provide investment returns superior to those achieved by the private accounts. Why? Since the funds are that organization's "public" account, it would be natural to assign the best managers to them. Also, the fact that those managers have almost 100 percent of their time available for management also helps explain the phenomenon. When you buy professional management via mutual funds, you get your money's worth.

INSULATION FROM CLIENT PRESSURES

When we consider how much time most account managers spend in face-to-face contact with clients, is it any wonder that such managers often fall victims to the pressures brought by their clients? One observer commented on this situation in June 1985 as follows:

> Dealing with mutual funds lowers the costs to sponsors of hiring and firing individual money managers and can ease the complications of personal relationships with local bank trust departments.[1]

Even though such managers may be resolute about their investment decisions, their willpower is subject to a breakdown when they are questioned by those who "pay the bills," that is, by the clients who pay their fees for management. Let us assume that a manager has invested a client's assets in a temporarily depressed stock. At a quarterly meeting with the client, the manager may point out that the stock's fundamentals remain favorable, thus making a case for retaining that stock in the portfolio. This tactic may work once, but what happens at a subsequent meeting with the client? Because of the pressure for short-term success, the manager may have to back away from his or her deeply felt convictions before the client's constant questioning. After all, we have to remember that "the client is always right."

By way of contrast, the "ivory tower" that protects mutual fund managers works to the advantage of the shareholders. Let us assume, for example, that an investor who receives a quarterly or semiannual report from a fund has a question concerning one of the investments in the portfolio. Except for isolated cases, that investor has

---

[1] Alan Krauss, "Mutual Funds Draw Interest," *Pensions & Investment Age,* June 10, 1985.

no way to apply pressure directly on the portfolio manager or to question him or her about why certain decisions were made. An investor who wishes to have a favorite stock included in the portfolio cannot question the portfolio manager about the reason for that stock's absence. Even if such an investor attends the annual meeting of the fund he or she still cannot raise the issue with the portfolio manager. While the officers of the fund will be at the meeting, the decision makers on individual portfolios will not necessarily be there. Thus portfolio managers of mutual funds are in an excellent position to make pressure-free decisions.

A DAILY RECORD OF PERFORMANCE

If your investments are managed by a bank trust department, a brokerage firm, or independent investment counselor, you will receive a monthly, quarterly, semiannual, or annual statement describing the activity in the account since the last report, current investments, and their total value. Many statements provide enough information so that you can easily compute the performance of your various holdings for different periods. But in the fast-moving marketplace of today, is such reporting really up-to-date? Let us assume that the market turns negative. Has the manager taken a defensive posture? The latest portfolio report may show a heavy concentration in automobile stocks, while newspaper articles report a sharp downturn in car sales. Has the adviser lightened up on those big positions? How is your portfolio doing in this tumultuous period?

Such nagging doubts do not exist if you invest in mutual funds. Just by reading the business-financial section of your daily newspaper, you can see how your funds are doing. Even if you have bought as many as 15 funds (a position we shall recommend later in this book), you can calculate their daily performance in only a few minutes. It's true that you cannot easily know about day-to-day changes in the composition of your portfolio. But if your funds continue to perform satisfactorily—which you can ascertain on a daily basis—why worry about such changes? Nervous investors, in particular, should welcome the peace of mind to be derived from their ability to have a daily performance check. (By contrast, some "trigger-happy" investors might be ill advised to invest in funds if day-to-day price swings might sway their long-term judgment about their investments.)

If you invest in mutual funds, you can easily gain a sense of their performance relative to the market as a whole or to alternative forms of investment. Many daily and weekly financial publications will help you track your funds' performance further by providing information on percentage changes along with closing prices and net asset values. Those who are not inclined to make such calculations will find that the statistical services, which we have previously mentioned, will fit the bill. In sum, you can have a professionally managed portfolio whose performance you can check in your daily newspaper.

FREEDOM FROM THE CHORE OF RECORD-KEEPING AND PAPERWORK

We all know how much time an individual investor with a diverse portfolio of stocks and bonds has to spend each year in keeping track of the paperwork on such items as purchases, sales, dividends, interest payments, stock splits, and tender offers. How long does it take portfolio managers at a bank or independent investment counseling firm to review each client's portfolio/activity summary, which has to reflect all the factors enumerated above? (An investment officer at an East Coast bank was honest enough to admit to me recently that because of the time constraints forced on him by the nature of broadly diversified stock and bond portfolios, he could review accounts of less than $250,000 only once a year.) Let us consider the problems confronting the head of operations or administration at such a firm. How many people and how much computer capability does such an officer need to enter, maintain, and print out all the various data and records of activity?

What if we could replace all that paperwork with a single "wrap-around" instrument that contained within its own operating structure all the required but laborious activity? Suppose that we only had to track a single or limited number of investments, and as a result we could cut down our administrative and operational overhead to a fraction of its former level.

Obviously we are not talking in theoretical terms; mutual funds provide the instrument. All the activity associated with diversified portfolios is collectivized through the mutual fund "shell." A fund owning 50 stocks might receive 200 quarterly dividends over the course of a year from these stocks, but the fund shareholder would receive only four dividend payments per year from the fund. This figure is the norm for most growth, balanced, and equity-income funds. Most of the aggressive growth funds make a single annual payment while income and bond funds have a monthly schedule of payments. If an investor normally turns over 50 percent of his or her portfolio each year, this would mean handling 25 purchases and 25 sales, plus calculating capital gains and losses on each sale. With a mutual fund, there are no purchases or sales to keep records on—except when you buy or sell shares of the fund itself. As for the calculations of capital gains and losses, most funds make a single such distribution per year. (This assumes there are net gains to be distributed; if the mutual fund had net losses for the fiscal year, no distribution is made.)

One word of caution is in order. If you reinvest your dividends and/or capital gain distributions for additional shares, you should keep accurate records of the tax base of the original shares and of any additional shares received in lieu of distributions.

Overall, whether we are speaking of an individual investor, a fiduciary for retirement plan assets, or professionals within investment management organizations, the dollar value of the time saved by investing in mutual funds is quite significant. Time is money, and mutual funds save time!

SAVINGS ON MANAGEMENT CHARGES

At this point let us consider three types of management charges that affect investors with portfolios of stocks and bonds. Our first example is an investor with a portfolio worth $250,000. Assume that this investor now wishes to add $5,000 or $10,000 to the portfolio. Even if the brokerage house were willing to negotiate the rate of its commission, it would still have to charge a higher rate for the purchase of a $5,000 or $10,000 investment than it did for the initial $250,000 investment.

A second example is a plan sponsor who is in the process of changing from one investment manager to another. How much of a commission will the plan sponsor have to pay to liquidate the portfolio assembled by the old manager? Again, how much of a commission has to be paid to accomplish all the purchases recommended by the new manager? In addition, what about the opportunity for profit that has been lost as a result of the time gap between the liquidation of the old portfolio and the establishment of the new one?

Our third example has to do with the yearly commissions paid by members of an investment policy group at a bank trust department or at an investment boutique. Do these investment managers realize how large the fees are? If we assume that these managers are associated with a small institution, that is, a bank or boutique that cannot negotiate down rates as easily as a large institution, then we can assume that these "excess" commissions will have a detrimental effect on the performance of their clients' investments.

All these problems affect only the purchasers of stocks and bonds, not those who invest in mutual funds. Thus we see that mutual funds provide a significant savings to investors on the costs of the administration, operation, and management of their portfolios.

RIGHTS OF ACCUMULATION

If you have invested in a load fund and desire to make a new purchase, your fund will take into consideration all your previous purchases in that particular family of funds in calculating the charge due on your current purchase. Thus if $250,000 has been invested in the fund in the past, and you wish to invest an additional $5,000 or $10,000, the fund would treat your investment as either $255,000 or $260,000 in calculating its sales charge. (You should keep in mind that the percentage of the sales charge diminishes as the size of the order increases.) But if you have invested in a no-load fund, you will incur no charges for additional purchases, no matter what the size of your order may be.

CUMULATIVE PURCHASE PRIVILEGES

There is another interesting feature to load funds as a group. If you purchase different amounts of shares of different funds in the group, all the purchases are lumped together in calculating the sales charges. Thus if you purchase $500,000 of the group's aggressive growth fund, $300,000 of its conservative growth fund, and $200,000 of its long-term, high-grade bond fund, the entire transaction would be treated as a single $1 million purchase. Keep in mind that for most fund groups, the sales charge at the million dollar level would be approximately 1 percent, while orders at the $200,000, $300,000, or $500,000 level would normally incur charges of between 2 and 5 percent.

EXCHANGE OR SWITCH PRIVILEGES

We have already mentioned this topic in Chapter Six, but it is worthwhile to repeat it once again at this point. Let us assume that your outlook in investing has changed, and that you wish to alter the composition of your portfolio. If there is a suitable range of alternatives within the fund group in which you have invested, you can accomplish a restructuring of your portfolio by switching to another fund with different objectives within that same group. The cost of exercising this privilege, which will be assessed by the fund's transfer agent, generally comes to about $5 per exchange.

It is only fair to point out here that some fund groups— in order to limit the disruptive effects of overly active market timers—have imposed a redemption charge for the sale of fund shares held less than a certain time. Other groups have limited the number of switches that can be made in a year at no incremental charge. All the same, we believe that your ability to alter the complexion of your investment portfolio for a charge of a mere $5 is a significant advantage. By itself it probably justifies the use of mutual funds in lieu of stocks and bonds. In contrast, there is no conceivable way for people to shuffle around a multimillion dollar stock and bond portfolio for just $5!

ADDITIONAL CONSIDERATIONS

You can save on investment costs of mutual funds in other ways as well. For example, fund ownership does not require you to receive (and file away in a safe place) share certificates. Instead, you will receive a simple book-entry notation from the fund's transfer agent. Periodically you and all the other shareholders will receive statements apprising you of your current share position and reflecting any recent activity in your account. A number of regulatory bodies have ruled that such statements will serve in lieu of the certificates required by fiduciaries to fulfill their custodial responsibility toward their clients.

Smaller investors will welcome another feature that has been alluded to briefly earlier in this chapter. Since mutual funds are very large purchasers of stocks and bonds, they can negotiate far more favorable commission rates with brokers. By being a part of this large pool of investment capital, individual investors and small institutions enjoy indirectly the benefit of much lower transaction costs.

To sum up, the advantages offered by mutual funds are quite attractive. Some features of the funds—like those we have just considered—have to do with the dollars-and-cents side of the business. Others involve features of a mental or psychological nature, such as the peace of mind afforded by the ability to check on one's investments and their performance on a daily basis. All these characteristics facilitate the investment process. They deserve the serious attention of all investors: small individual investors, corporate officers responsible for the retirement plan assets of their firms, investment officers at trust banks, and principals in investment counseling firms.

* * *

There are distinct and positive advantages to all types of investors in mutual funds. As an industry, funds are experiencing a phase of dynamic growth. Their suitability for investors has been legitimized. Many features of the funds are subject to governmental regulation. As a result, funds are able to overcome many problems facing today's investors. Because of their liquidity and compactness, they allow investors to move as quickly as present-day markets. Because of the range of their offerings, investors have the flexibility to capture a wide portion of the newly expanded spectrum of the investment market. In addition, the ancillary benefits of an operational, administrative, and financial nature strengthen the argument in favor of the funds.

At this point we are ready to take the mutual fund concept to its final stage. We shall no longer consider the funds as an investment by themselves, but rather as building blocks in an investment strategy—pieces of a well-thought-out and soundly constructed portfolio that can deliver safe, consistent, and above-average returns, despite the direction of the market and the objectives of the investors! This is multifund investing, the subject of Part Three.

Multifund Investing

The Investment Pyramid

NEWFANGLED PORTFOLIO THEOREMS

As we have seen, the investment world has become a difficult place, and most investors have become skeptical of the old-fashioned, seat-of-the-pants approach to investments. Therefore, it is not surprising that a new school of thought has developed. Its followers would have us believe that the individual investment manager cannot bring value-added to the process. Instead, a rigidly dogmatic approach is suggested. Under the banner of "modern portfolio theory," some of these theorists categorize stocks and bonds under such terms as *alphas* and *betas*. Investors are asked to decide on their risk-tolerance level, examine the historical risk characteristics of each issue, mix them in the proper proportion, and then *presto*—an instant portfolio is born!

Discourses on such portfolio theorems run into the hundreds of pages. Even certain sections of academe are getting into the act. Weighty journals now abound to provide scholarly dissertations on various aspects of the "science" of investment management. We live in the age of computers, so why shouldn't we believe that investment portfolios can be custom-made by computer like virtually everything else today? What is improbable about creating the CAD-CAM of Wall Street?

I for one do not accept this "new religion." The method we will describe in the following pages is based on a simple, straightforward approach that has been tried and successfully tested for over 10 years. You do not need an advanced degree in computer technology to understand it, nor do you need to read hundreds of pages of explanation because it consists of only four basic steps. As many an observer has commented, this approach appears to follow the KISS method (Keep It Simple, Stupid).

We are often asked, "If your method is so simple, why do many so-called experts seek to confuse the issue with complicated, hard-to-understand methods?" I have no solid answer other than the observation that if such methods do not deliver the projected results, their proponents can always "hide behind the computer" to explain their errors. Perhaps these people fear that simplicity would not allow them to rationalize their annual six-figure retainers. If the clients clearly understand what's going on—or feel that they can handle their investments by themselves—the rationale for high consulting and management fees might be in jeopardy. As a result, the so-called experts create layer upon layer of investment "technology," regression analysis, and standard deviations. They especially keep in mind the fact that "an ignorant client is the best client."

THE RIGHT SOLUTION: THE INVESTMENT PYRAMID

Let me now call to your attention the investment pyramid depicted in Figure 8–1. The entire process of portfolio construction consists of just four steps. We will examine each of these steps in greater detail in the following chapters. At this point we want to give a quick overview of the pyramid. Even a cursory glance at Figure 8–1 shows that we are dealing here with a method of building portfolios that proceeds from the top downward. Step 1, at the top of the pyramid, involves objective setting; Step 2, asset allocation; Step 3, sector allocation; and Step 4, mutual fund selection. Each step leads naturally to the next one.

The process goes from the general to the specific. We begin with a very basic concept of what we want from our investments; we add the necessary details; and we end up with a fully structured portfolio. As we shall see later, the linkage between these steps is truly from the top downward. Changes at a step higher up on the pyramid

FIGURE 8–1   The Investment Pyramid

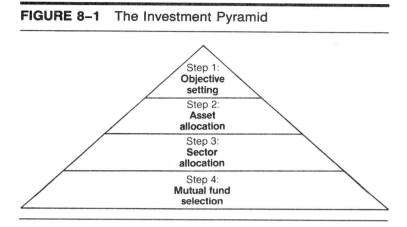

automatically force changes in the step or steps below, but not vice versa.

From another perspective this process is like a building project. Admittedly, this building is unusual in that it is being constructed from the top downward. But as if we were constructing a building, we would start with an "artist's rendition," that is, by setting our investment objectives. Next we would develop more detailed "line drawings," that is, we allocate our assets. Then we would draw up "engineering plans" or allocate the sectors of our portfolio. Finally, we would "put up the structure," that is, we select our mutual funds. Steps One to Three are like a building structure to which we have to add "bricks and mortar," namely, the mutual funds selected for the portfolio. Keep in mind that any building of unsound structure to which we add quality materials would be doomed in advance to failure. The same would be true if we were to apply subpar bricks and mortar to a building with a sturdy framework. We need to pay careful attention to details at every step of the investment process.

Additional features of this four-step process bear further study. The first is obvious: As our building blocks we have replaced stocks and bonds with a carefully selected group of mutual funds. The reason for this decision is by now quite clear. In today's investment environment stocks and bonds can be likened to subpar materials.

THE PROPER EMPHASIS

Next comes the question of emphasis. In the traditional approach stock and bond selection is such a time-consuming process that little time is left over to set our objectives, allocate our assets, and allocate sectors of our portfolio. As we shall see in the next four chapters, mutual fund selection—the substitute for stock and bond selection—is perhaps the least time-consuming step of all if it is done properly. This allows us to focus our attention on the critical Steps One through Three.

These steps are critical because a number of studies have clearly shown that the most effective use of a portfolio manager's time is spent on asset and sector allocation, not on stock and bond selection! One study, in fact, concluded that over 60 percent of the incremental returns provided by a group of investment managers was the result of proper asset and sector allocation. Less than 10 percent could be attributed to correct stock and bond selection. (The balance is accounted for by miscellaneous factors.) Success with one's portfolio has little to do with selecting individual issues. Every rule has its exception, and this one is no different. Yes, there are disciples of Graham & Dodd—those well-known advocates of investing in basic value stocks—who spend 100 percent of their time on stock selection, and do so very successfully. But they are the exception.

Although it may be hard for us at first to accept the fact that the selection of stocks and bonds plays only a minor role in successful investing, let us consider the following situation: When the market declines, as it did between 1973 and 1974 and between 1981 and August 1982, how might portfolio managers have better spent their time? Should they have decided whether to own stock in General Motors Corporation or Ford Motor Company? U. S. Steel or Bethlehem Steel? Philip Morris Incorporated or R. J. Reynolds Tobacco Co.? Alternatively, shouldn't they have decided whether to be in equities at all or in cash equivalents? From the late 1970s to the early 1980s, while interest rates were rising precipitously, how did the bond managers better spend their time—researching various credits of the same rating and similar maturities, or by determining whether to be at the long end of the interest rate curve or at the short end? The evidence and logic are clearly in favor of asset and sector allocation, not stock and bond selection.

In a rising market most securities appreciate in value; in a declining market the reverse is true. Finding miniscule differences between different issues in either environment is futile. Portfolio managers who correctly spent their time on asset allocation between January 1973 and September 1974, and who determined to stay out of the stock market completely, would have outperformed the most astute stock picker who determined to stay fully invested during this period. By shifting the emphasis away from stock and bond selection and toward portfolio construction, the investment pyramid forces a focus on the critical steps.

TWO TEAMS OF SPECIALISTS: PORTFOLIO MANAGERS AND MUTUAL FUND MANAGERS

Finally, perhaps the most noteworthy characteristic of this four-step process is the development of a new notion.

What we see here is a breaking out of separate and distinct investment functions. On the first level there is portfolio management, the proper structuring of the overall portfolio. On the second level we have stock and bond selection. However, each is a full-time undertaking. Those attempting to fulfill both roles simultaneously, particularly in a volatile, complex marketplace, are doomed to failure. Each role requires the total devotion of the practitioner. Instead, what we propose here is something quite different. Portfolio managers, or individual investors, who until now have attempted to wear both hats, will give up one hat. They will perform the function we now call portfolio management, or portfolio design, and when it is time to perform the second function—stock and bond selection—they will call upon a second group of professionals, the mutual fund managers, to whom we will delegate this responsibility. The portfolio manager, rid of the responsibility of selecting stocks and bonds, can tap the expertise of a 1,300-member farm team of stock and bond fund managers to perform this role for him.

As I wrote in a 1984 article in the *American Banker:*

> This farming out should not take on a negative connotation, but rather a very positive one. Typically, the individual portfolio manager can at best devote only a few minutes per day to any of the myriad number of investment sectors that have developed into full-time enterprises in recent years, such as options, convertible bonds, medical technology, etc. By delegating the stock and bond selection process, we now have a portfolio manager who can call upon the services of a group of carefully selected specialty mutual fund managers who devote 100 percent of their time focused solely on their areas of specialization.[1]

---

[1]Michael D. Hirsch, "Mutual Funds: Key to Investment Management," *American Banker,* April 16, 1984.

That is the crucial link—two teams of specialists consisting of portfolio managers and mutual fund managers who work in tandem to the ultimate benefit of the investor. Each team devotes itself full-time to its area of expertise, with no duplication of effort! Portfolio managers spend none of their time on stock and bond selection; mutual fund managers spend none of theirs on objective setting or asset and sector allocation. Again, a rule with exceptions. There are a number of mutual funds that perform active asset allocation, but they are an extremely small minority.

Step One: Objective Setting

"KNOW THYSELF"

As we indicated in Figure 8–1, the first step in putting together a sound portfolio has little to do with portfolio construction, but it is perhaps the most critical step of all. Improperly performed, it dooms the rest of the process to failure. Proper objective setting is paramount. As the stock exchanges implore brokers to "know the customer," so here—whether one is an individual or professional investor—the exhortation must be, *"Know thyself!"* We must dissuade ourselves or our clients from unrealistic notions.

Without a clear picture of yourself or your clients, there is absolutely no way to design a sound portfolio. What type of individual is the investor? What are his or her investment goals? Is the interest primarily in current income, long-term capital appreciation, or some combination of the two? For instance, an investor requiring a high level of current income cannot be enticed by the spectacular returns of aggressive growth funds during bull markets. Most such funds provide little or no current income (not to mention the irreparable capital loss that would be suffered if the market went down). If current income is the goal, preserving the capital base from which that income is generated is crucial.

More important, *how much risk is the investor willing to absorb in return for how much reward?* There is no getting away from that most basic of investment principles: the greater the risk, the greater the potential reward. There is no shortage of investment hucksters out there touting the latest "risk-free" investment—a potential of 30 to 40 percent in annual returns with no downside. What an attractive offer! But if it were real, the vendor could have become independently wealthy long ago by investing his or her own money in this offering. Unfortunately, that is not the real world.

I cannot enumerate the number of potential clients who have entered my office with the same investment goal: maximum return and minimum risk. If I were only able to deliver such a product or service! The process, then, begins by causing the individual to focus on reality. Let us suppose the investor is interested in maximum growth, and is willing to absorb a high degree of risk in return for a rate of return far above average. What if we encounter another period like 1973–74? Is the investor prepared to see his or her capital depreciate by 50 to 60 percent? (Some "go-go" mutual funds actually declined by over 80 percent in that dreadful period.) Are investors prepared to sit back and watch their $100,000 investment shrink to $50,000 or $40,000? After such soul-searching questioning it is amazing how the list of maximum growth investors has shrunk. But there is no getting away from it: the more of a reward is sought, the greater is the risk investors must be willing to bear.

THE LONG–TERM FRAMEWORK

When we embark on Step One, it is important to keep our sights on the long term. Objective setting is not a short-term exercise. We are not trying to determine what is expected from investments over the next six months, but rather what are our goals in three to five years.

If I tell a prospective client that my growth-and-income clients have achieved annualized returns of 15 percent for the past 10 years, and that prospect asks me what assurances I can give that his or her account will be up 15 percent six months from now, my answer is simple: none! Particularly because of the erratic nature of investment markets today, no one can guarantee with any degree of certainty where events will take us in as short a period as six months.

It is unfair to make such a request of an investment

manager, and it is unrealistic for an investor to expect such a performance of himself or herself. If your objectives are set intelligently and given enough time, they can be met. An exception must be made for unusual circumstances, for example, when objectives might be changed more than once a year. Otherwise, the investment process is being mishandled through such frequent changes.

THE DISTINCTION BETWEEN SAVINGS AND INVESTMENTS

One other proviso: a clear line of delineation must be drawn between *savings* and *investments*. Too many individuals confuse the two. Just because a portion of the investment portfolio is kept liquid does not mean that you are fulfilling your need for savings. Far from it! Such a cash reserve fulfills an investment function (as a buying reserve or as a source of risk-free current income); it does not fulfill a savings function.

In classical terms the need for savings must be satisfied before any dollars become available for investment. Savings come first. They are the "rainy day" fund, the pool of capital that absolutely *must* be available in case of an emergency. There are many formulas as to how much savings are needed, but a general rule of thumb is six months to a year. In other words, if all other sources of income were cut off, how much would be available for living expenses for the next 6 to 12 months? That is the role savings play. By their very nature they cannot be subjected to any risk of capital loss at all! If calculations show that one requires $100,000 in savings, we must be completely certain that if a "rainy day" arrives, $100,000 will be available. Very few investments offer such certainty.

Assuming, then, that the savings function has been

TABLE 9-1   Five Investment Options

Objective	Risk Factor	Fund Medium
Variable rate of current income without principal fluctuation	Extremely low	Bank and short-term Treasury instruments
Fixed rate of current income with capital appreciation potential	Moderate to high, based on interest rate trends	Income portfolio
Current income with some capital growth potential	Moderate	Balanced portfolio
Long-term capital and income growth	Moderate to high	Growth portfolio
Maximum capital growth with little or no dividend income	High to very high	Aggressive growth portfolio

---

fulfilled, the balance of available capital can be considered free for investment. If we have gone through the soul-searching process of setting objectives described above, we are now prepared to begin designing a suitable portfolio. Table 9-1 is a "map" that will help steer the investor's or fiduciary's thinking into one of four fairly well defined paths. (The first of the five options in Table 9-1 describes a savings function, not investments.) A number of permutations exist, but personal experience has shown that over 90 percent of all investors can be slotted into one of the other four categories.

THE RISK FACTOR

The description of the risk factor accurately reflects the reality of today's marketplace. Going from an income-oriented objective to one primarily focused on long-term growth normally entails absorbing a higher level of risk. But because of the wide fluctuations in interest rates we have observed in recent years, fixed-income instruments are as subject to capital loss as are equities and similar investments. So in setting objectives, we cannot automatically assume what the funding medium will be. As we shall see in the next two chapters, if we project sharply higher interest rates, the risk level in an income portfolio funded primarily through long-term bonds would be very high. Conversely, if you are predicting lower interest rates, then the risk level of a maximum growth portfolio funded to some degree with long-term bonds would be substantially lower than the risk level of a portfolio funded entirely with small, emerging growth stocks.

Table 9–1 helps qualify the trade-offs involved in objective setting. The greater the emphasis on growth, the higher will be the risk. Also, any attempt to improve growth possibilities must come at the expense of current income. We will explore one aspect of this concept shortly, but for now you must realize that this is an inviolate investment axiom. A portfolio structured to provide current income can only provide so much in the way of growth possibilities. Conversely, a portfolio designed for maximum growth can only supply a very small amount of current income. Again, every rule has its exception, and if we were fortunate enough to purchase long-term high-coupon bonds just prior to a precipitous drop in interest rates, we would enjoy a fine rate of current income and capital appreciation as well. Unfortunately, in order to convert those unrealized capital gains into realized gains, we would have to sell the high-coupon bonds. The new ones purchased in their place would offer a much less attractive interest rate.

BEWARE OF FADS!

One additional warning: beware of fads! Particularly if your focus is firmly aimed at the long term, as suggested above, this should be easy. But we have encountered too many investors easily swayed by the latest rage to take this warning lightly. How many investors, regardless of their objectives, were "trapped" by the lure of the high-technology funds in the first half of 1983? Because of the subsequent slide in the technology area, it will take years before such investors will be able to recoup their initial investment, let alone fulfill their original objectives.

How many investors are aimlessly investing today in the latest fad: "government securities yield plus" funds? Are these funds meant for all the investors who are investing in them? How many of these people realize that the yields on the funds are enhanced by writing options on the portfolio's positions? If interest rates decline, these positions will be called away by those who purchased the options and will have to be replaced by lower-coupon issues. If rates rise, the total value of the portfolio will decline as current holdings are "marked to the market."

Such are the enticements—the mythical sirens—of the investment world. More so than perhaps in any other sphere of activity, it seems that investors are under constant pressure to get into something "new and different." True, when the stock market is sharply rising, returns on aggressive growth funds will look particularly attractive, but if your primary objective is current income, do not be led astray! Aggressive growth funds provide little or no current income. Or if your primary objective is long-term growth, do not be lured by bond funds that have enhanced their yield by writing options on their portfolio. They have no chance of providing capital appreciation.

THE SO-CALLED RISK-FREE INVESTMENTS

Finally, a word about so-called risk-free investments. Investors often ask, "Why should I absorb any risk at all, particularly if I am an income-oriented investor? I'll simply buy 30-year Treasuries, get a steady rate of income, and have my principal guaranteed by the U.S. government!" It seems like a foolproof argument except for two factors that can hardly be described as minor.

First, what if circumstances force you to sell those bonds before they reach maturity? Few if any investors can say with complete assurance that their objectives or lifestyle will not change sometime in the next 20 to 30 years. The government (or bank) guarantees your principal only if it is held to maturity. If for some reason you have to sell your bonds prior to maturity, and if interest rates have risen in the interim, you will receive far less than your original investment. If interest rates have risen far enough, any interest income will be more than offset by capital losses. To check on this statement, just ask anyone who invested in bonds between 1945 and 1982!

Second, what about inflation? The cornerstone of any investment program is to preserve the purchasing power of the invested dollars. When you liquidate your investments to use the proceeds for whatever purpose you originally had in mind (for example, paying for a child's college expenses or as a retirement benefit), you should be able to realize an equal dollar amount of goods and services at that time as when you first invested the monies. If you make an investment to fund your child's college expenses in 10 to 20 years, the current tuition charges are not relevant. What really matters is what these charges will probably be when your child is ready to enter college.

WHAT ABOUT INFLATION?

If we lived in a zero-inflation environment, the guesswork over such planning would be miniscule. Tuitions in 10 to 20 years would approximate current levels. But the harsh lessons of the 1970s and early 80s have taught us a bitter lesson about investment planning in a period of high inflation. It does not matter what the absolute returns on investment are but rather what the net adjusted returns are after inflation. If the value of a portfolio rose by 10 percent, while inflation rose by 11 percent, the investor would have lost money in terms of purchasing power!

As Table 9–2 highlights, inflation is perhaps the most difficult hurdle of all to overcome in an investment program. Let us assume that you invest a dollar for 30 years at a time when inflation averages only 5 percent per year. Judging by recent experience, one would call that a period of low inflation. But your original dollar would only be worth *23 cents* in purchasing power at the end of that time. Relate that now to the "risk-free" investor who owns long-term U.S. Treasuries. At an average annual inflation rate of 5 percent, $1,000 invested in a 30-year Treasury would be worth no more than $230, inflation-adjusted, on redemption.

Thus the message of all this is quite clear: even the most risk-averse investors must achieve sufficient capital growth to overcome the forces of inflation. A portfolio with no possibilities of growth can never achieve your desired objectives—no matter how conservative they may be—so long as we continue to live in an inflationary environment. The amount of growth to be sought—even for the most conservative investors—has to be linked to the inflation levels that are predicted. If you project an inflation rate of 5 percent, your portfolio must grow 5 percent per year to remain intact. What if the inflation rate rises to 10 percent? Then you will have to have a 10 percent growth rate.

TABLE 9-2 What $1 Will Be Worth (average annual rate of inflation)

Years from Today	3%	4%	5%	6%	7%	8%	9%	10%	11%	12%	15%	18%	20%
5	$0.86	$0.82	$0.78	$0.75	$0.71	$0.68	$0.65	$0.62	$0.59	$0.57	$0.50	$0.44	$0.40
6	0.84	0.79	0.75	0.70	0.67	0.63	0.60	0.56	0.53	0.51	0.43	0.37	0.33
7	0.81	0.76	0.71	0.67	0.62	0.58	0.55	0.51	0.48	0.45	0.38	0.31	0.28
8	0.79	0.73	0.68	0.63	0.58	0.54	0.50	0.47	0.43	0.40	0.33	0.27	0.23
9	0.77	0.70	0.64	0.59	0.54	0.50	0.46	0.42	0.39	0.36	0.28	0.23	0.19
10	0.74	0.68	0.61	0.56	0.51	0.46	0.42	0.39	0.35	0.32	0.25	0.19	0.16
15	0.64	0.56	0.48	0.42	0.36	0.32	0.27	0.24	0.21	0.18	0.12	0.08	0.06
20	0.55	0.46	0.38	0.31	0.26	0.21	0.18	0.15	0.12	0.10	0.06	0.04	0.03
25	0.48	0.38	0.30	0.23	0.18	0.15	0.12	0.09	0.07	0.06	0.03	0.02	0.01
30	0.41	0.31	0.23	0.17	0.13	0.10	0.08	0.06	0.04	0.03	0.02	0.01	—
35	0.36	0.25	0.18	0.13	0.09	0.07	0.05	0.04	0.03	0.02	0.01	—	—
40	0.31	0.21	0.14	0.10	0.07	0.05	0.03	0.02	0.02	0.01	—	—	—
45	0.26	0.17	0.11	0.07	0.05	0.03	0.02	0.01	0.01	—	—	—	—
50	0.23	0.14	0.09	0.05	0.03	0.02	0.01	0.01	0.01	—	—	—	—

SOURCE: *UNITED Mutual Fund Selector*, 210 Newbury Street, Boston, Mass. 02116. *UNITED Mutual Fund Selector* is a twice-monthly publication of United Business Service Company, sold at a $98 annual subscription rate.

* * *

Let us now sum up the basics of objective setting:

1. "Know thyself."
2. Maintain a long-term framework.
3. Define your risk-reward parameters.
4. Differentiate between your savings and your investments.
5. Beware of fads.
6. Remember that there are no risk-free investments.

Now that we have clearly defined our objectives, we can proceed to Step Two—asset allocation—and to Step Three—sector allocation.

Steps Two and Three:
Asset Allocation and
Sector Allocation

Once investment objectives are clearly defined, we can embark upon the process of constructing a portfolio. Remember that we are keeping things simple, and that we will go from the general to the specific. In that sense asset allocation is the framework on which we will build the remainder of the process.

True, a number of extremely "sophisticated" models of asset allocation are available today—models that provide reams of output and require advanced computer expertise to run and understand. Also, most of these models are based solely on past experience. If one presumes the future will exactly duplicate the past, one can believe, as these systems do, that there is a "90 percent degree of assurance" that the desired investment objectives will be met. But at best this is a highly vacuous assumption. No system can give the user any degree of assurance that x percent in stocks, y percent in bonds, z percent in cash, and q percent in real estate will give you an n percent return with no single year below an m percent return.

STEP TWO: ASSET ALLOCATION

Let us proceed instead with a simple, straightforward approach. In our method asset allocation will consist of the following questions: *In view of the now-determined investment objectives, and with some notion of market trends in the next six to nine months, what percent of assets should we target for growth-oriented investments? What percent should we allocate to income-oriented investments and what percent should remain liquid?* That is the entire process: allocating your assets for growth, income, or liquidity. It is no more complicated than that.

Obviously, some notion of where the markets are headed depends on the type of investor we are talking about. If until now you have relied on advice from stockbrokers, friends, or independent research to develop a sense of the investment climate, you will have to continue relying on such sources to develop a sense of the future climate. Institutional investors—bank trust officers and investment counselors, for example—normally have internal capabilities (supported by external research inputs) to make such determinations. The fiduciary or plan sponsor looks to consultants or advisers to develop a sense of market trends.

There are widely divergent ways to develop such a sense. On the one hand is the school of technical analysts who believe that the markets travel along well-defined patterns. They hold that by plotting these courses and following certain preconceived rules, we can determine the future direction of the markets. Another school—the fundamentalists—believes that the direction of the markets is a function of basic economic, political, and monetary factors. What is happening on the international and domestic political scenes that might have an impact on future values? What do current trends in the money supply, exchange rates, and actions of the Federal Reserve Board lead us to believe about the future value of the dollar and the impact of such developments on interest rates? Finally, in looking at current economic developments, where do we stand in the economic cycle? Does it seem that the period ahead will be in a phase of expansion or of contraction?

It is not the purpose of this book to judge the relative merits of the technical and fundamentalist schools as well as their different approaches to the creation of investment scenarios. There are persuasive arguments for and against each school. Proponents of each approach can apply the proposed four-step process to portfolio building. For the sake of example let us now presume that you use the fundamental approach.

We will suppose that you are primarily seeking

growth, with current income as a secondary consideration. A fundamental analysis of the current situation has convinced you that we are in an expansionary economic phase, with only minor storm clouds on the political and monetary horizons. If this is the case, you would want to create a bullish asset allocation, with some measure of restraint (to reflect the uncertainties). Following the growth-income-liquid approach to asset allocation, you might allocate 65 percent of your assets to growth-oriented investments, 30 percent to income-oriented investments, and retain 5 percent in liquid investments (as a hedge and buying reserve, or as a source of low-risk returns when short-term interest rates are high). The overall mix reflects an inherently bullish posture. The particular mix reflects a portfolio geared toward growth, but with a secondary focus on income generation.

What if later your lingering concerns over monetary and political policies diminish? Result: You need to adjust your asset allocation accordingly. Perhaps now your allocation will be 75 percent for growth-oriented investments, 20 percent for income-oriented investments, and 5 percent to remain liquid. Why do you have 20 percent in income-oriented investments when the outlook is so bullish? Conversely, why don't you have 100 percent in growth investments? There are two answers to these questions. First, nothing is ever so sure that you as an investor would want all your assets in one basket, even on the level of asset allocation. Investments that generate income are generally better hedges against a downside reversal because their income level acts as a better cushion than that provided by growth investments. Second, since current income is a secondary objective, it cannot be sacrificed, however bullish the scenario.

Time has passed, and now the recovery appears to be over. As we experienced in mid-1983, the Federal Reserve Board may restrict monetary growth out of fear of an

TABLE 10-1   Asset Allocation (objective: growth)

Sentiment	Growth	Income	Liquid
Very bullish	75%	20%	5%
Bullish	65	30	5
Neutral	50	35	15
Somewhat bearish	35	35	30
Very bearish	10	10	80

overheating economy, or Congress may pass legislation you fear the market will read as antigrowth. Your allocation must now be shifted to a more conservative posture. As a growth investor, your allocation should perhaps now be 50 percent for growth, 35 percent for income, and 15 percent for liquidity. If your readings of the environment subsequently become more ominous, your investments should be 35 percent, growth; 35 percent, income; and 30 percent, liquid. If you envision a repeat of the 1973-74 experience, then your allocation should be 10 percent, growth; 10 percent, income; and 80 percent, liquid.

Table 10-1 carries a twofold message. First, the recommended approach is totally fluid; nothing is chiseled in stone. Particularly in the current volatile environment, an asset allocation that is developed and then "stored away" may work for a while, but it will eventually backfire. Your allocation must change as often as events do. Remember, though, that we are taking an intermediate-to long-term perspective. Attempts to capture short-term swings by constant reallocations will create unnecessary trading expenses and "whipsaws" as the investors start buying when they should be selling, and vice versa. Market timing geared to capturing short-term swings in the market will eventually fail. Over 10 years of experience has shown that significant changes in allocations need not occur more frequently than once every 9 to 12 months, with some fine-tuning in between. On the other hand, taking a longer perspective than 12 months is also fruitless because of the current speed with which events change.

Second, investors should enter this allocation process with no preconceived notions. Because you view yourself as having a growth objective does not necessarily mean you must always have the vast majority of your assets invested in growth-oriented investments. Let us assume that the environment is not conducive to growth, as is the case during a deep recession. If you are stubborn and keep the bulk of your assets in growth-oriented investments, you may derive some sort of psychic pleasure because you are fortunate enough to lose less than everyone else. But this does little for your asset base! Your objective is a long-term goal. If short-term events do not bode well for achieving that goal, then the objective must be temporarily tabled and replaced by one that stresses capital preservation. Successful investing is not based on the concept of "my objective, right or wrong."

Finally, you need to pay attention to the terminology we have used. Notice we speak of *growth and income*, not of *stocks and bonds* or of *equity and debt.* Why? Very simply because in today's investment atmosphere, the last-named two sets of items don't accurately describe asset allocation. True, in the 1950s and 60s investors determined the emphasis their portfolios should have on growth, which became the percentage invested in stocks. The portion of the portfolio devoted to income was automatically invested in bonds.

All of this was fine as long as interest rates hardly ever budged. Stocks were the way to achieve growth, and bonds were a safe way to provide income. Not today! With the stock market so volatile, and with the bond market shifting as quickly as once only stocks did, a new terminology and a new perspective are required. When interest rates fall rapidly, bonds, especially lower-graded ones, may be a more likely source of growth than stocks. In fact, between 1982 and 1985 most high-yield bond funds provided a greater total return than the majority of aggressive growth funds. Conversely, if interest rates rise rapidly, stocks with high dividend rates or short-term money market instruments might be a better way to provide current income than long-term bonds.

Yes, there are times when we want to be invested in stocks (equities) or in bonds (debts). But that is a determination to be made on the level of sector allocation, not of asset allocation. On the first level of portfolio construction, our focus is strictly on growth-income-liquid.

We have now reached the halfway point in the process of multifund investing. Our investment objectives have been determined as well as our long-term goals. We have surveyed the political, economic, and monetary situations, or we have studied the technical charts and reached conclusions as to how all these factors bode for investments over the coming 9 to 12 months. On the basis of these findings, we have drawn up a simple, straightforward asset allocation plan. We have created a list of growth-oriented investments, income-oriented investments, and liquid investments that will act as a basis for the rest of the process of portfolio building. We have begun the framework; now it is time to add detail, namely, to make our sector allocation.

STEP THREE: SECTOR ALLOCATION

At this point let us recall again the investment pyramid in Figure 8–1. Multifund investing starts with a kernel of an idea at the top of the pyramid, objective setting. Slowly but surely the process expands until we reach, at the base of the pyramid, our completed portfolio. Step Three—

sector allocation—is the last stage before we apply the "bricks and mortar" to our building process, that is to say, before we purchase mutual funds for the portfolio.

A word of warning is in order here. When we speak about *sectors,* we are speaking of sectors in the overall investment market, *not* stock market sectors. Particularly today, this distinction is critical because of the marketing thrust given to *sector funds.* These are funds whose investments are limited to stocks in a specific industry group or related series of groups, such as finance, medicine, insurance, and defense. The assumption is made that an investor has the qualifications to perform all the tasks one would normally expect of a mutual fund manager, except for stock selection. This is such an aberration of the basic concept of mutual funds that we hope that it will prove to be a short-lived fad.

An article in a 1985 issue of *Business Week* pointed out:

> Betting on the past performance of a specialty, or "sector," fund can prove dangerous, however. For one thing, these funds violate the principles of diversification that the funds themselves have long preached. More important, hot stock groups often make the major part of their move in a short time. After that they tend to languish. Picking a fund whose specialty has already been discovered by the smart money and has made it to the front of the mutual fund pack is likely to be a losing strategy. Indeed, 8 of 1985's 12 worst performers are specialized funds. . . . If you lose money because you picked the wrong sector fund, however, you can't blame an inept portfolio manager—only yourself.[1]

Sector allocation as used in this text, therefore, refers to something completely different. Our sectors are sub-

---

[1] Jeffrey M. Laderman, "Why 'Specialty' Funds Are Risky Business," *Business Week,* July 22, 1985.

sets within the general categories previously outlined as growth, income, and liquid. To see how this works, each asset class must be examined independently. You should keep in mind that a far more compact time frame will be used than the one we used for asset allocation.

Growth Investments

Let us take up first the assets we intend to target for growth investments. After considering the conditions we expect to find in the stock market over the next three to six months, *what percent of our assets should be in aggressive growth investments? What percentage should be in conservative growth investments?* It is no more complex than that. Of course, we might want to add some finer permutations, such as the possibility of using superaggressive funds (that is, funds which were more than 85 percent invested in high-tech issues in early 1983, or sector funds in high-risk areas like medical technology). But for all intents and purposes, the distinction between aggressive growth investments and conservative growth investments is as far as we need go.

The beauty of this interplay with asset allocation is the flexibility it provides. For instance, if your opinion of the equity market has improved somewhat, but not to the degree that a shift in asset allocation is called for, you simply need to shift the balance between aggressive growth and conservative growth more toward the aggressive side, and you will achieve the desired effect. The reverse is obviously also true. If you become slightly more pessimistic, but not sufficiently so to reduce your asset allocation to growth, then you can move somewhat from aggressive growth to conservative growth on the sector level.

Income Investments

Let us now take up the second category within sector allocation: income investments. *In view of the short- to intermediate-term prospects for the stock and bond markets, do you prefer to derive your income from either equity-income sources or fixed-income sources?* (Equity-income funds provide a high rate of current income by overweighting their portfolios with shares of companies with high dividend rates.) Note that your determination of the relative prospects between the stock and bond markets decides your allocation within this sector. If you expect flat or lower interest rates, you will probably prefer fixed-income sources. All the same, you might keep a percentage of your allocation in equity income if you expect the stock market to rise as well over this period. Conversely, if you expect higher interest rates, you might prefer equity-income sources. Of course, if you expect a severe decline in both the stock and bond markets as a result of sharply higher rates, you will want to shift your allocation of assets. You will downgrade income investments in favor of liquid investments.

Again, further permutations are possible, specifically in defining the sector allocation to fixed-income sources: Will the bond funds selected have long-term, intermediate-term, or short-term maturities? Will their portfolios contain high-grade issues, low-grade issues, such as junk bond funds or high-yield funds, or a mixture of all these issues? Will the debentures in the portfolio trade near par, or will they be deep-discount issues? Will the portfolio contain straight debt issues, convertibles, or a combination of the two? Will the fund invest in taxable issues or be tax-free? Will the fund focus on the new breed of debt issues, such as GNMAs and zero-coupons?

Some attention should also be given to the relative merits of tax-free bond funds, as this is a choice of an ever-larger number of investors. As we pointed out in Chapter Five, there was only a handful of such funds just a few years ago—so few, in fact, that they were not even classified separately. Now the business sections of our newspapers and financial publications are overrun with oversized advertisements touting the merits of this fund group's general tax-free fund, or that group's state tax-free (or double-exempt) fund, or a third group's insured tax-free fund.

The question remains: Are these funds right for you as an investor? Remember, I warned you earlier not to let your long-term objectives be swayed by short-term fads or crazes. Just because it was determined in Step One that your objective was primarily current income or a combination of income and growth, it does not necessarily follow that the best after-tax returns are available from tax-free funds. It is shortsighted of you as an investor to accept the lower yields provided by tax-free funds instead of the higher returns derived from taxable funds for no other reason than your reluctance to pay taxes on your income.

As Table 10–2 indicates, you must know your tax bracket to judge the suitability of tax-free funds. Let us look, for instance, at someone in a 30 percent tax bracket. If long-term taxable bond funds yield 13 percent, and long-term tax-free funds only yield 9 percent, it pays to invest in the taxable bond fund; the net after-tax yield would be higher. Individuals in the 50 percent tax bracket investing in a tax-free money market fund yielding 4.5 percent would be better off on an after-tax basis with that lower yield than if they had chosen a taxable money fund paying 8.5 percent. I strongly urge clients and students to keep information like that in Table 10–2 readily available in considering tax-free investments. Similar tables

TABLE 10–2   Tax-Free/Taxable
Equivalents*

Tax-Free Yield	30 Percent Bracket	40 Percent Bracket	50 Percent Bracket
4.00%	5.71%	6.67%	8.00%
4.50	6.43	7.50	9.00
6.00	8.57	10.00	12.00
8.00	11.42	13.33	16.00
9.00	12.86	15.00	18.00
10.00	14.29	16.66	20.00

*Based on the 1983 federal tax schedules.

include the effect of state and local taxes for states that, in effect, have a double tax on interest and dividend income.

Even investors from states with high state withholding taxes should be wary of a number of pitfalls regarding double-exempt tax-free funds. As a 1985 article by John Heins in *Forbes Magazine* pointed out:

> Sounds good for double-exempt funds. But don't let the lure of the extra tax exemption cloud your judgment. Because of rate differentials between states, a national muni bond fund, exempt from only federal income taxes, could be a better buy.... [Ed.: Mr. Heins is speaking of a Massachusetts double-exempt load fund.] The Massachusetts exemption will be worth only about 0.5 percent annually to a high bracket investor, meaning that it could take eight years to earn back what is lost in the sales commission.... Another problem with the double-exempt funds: You give up flexibility and geographic diversification.... Investing in just one state can be a risky proposition. Hard times hit different regions and states unevenly.... Double-exempt funds are a good idea, but not for investors who buy blindly.[2]

[2] John Heins, "Double Whammy," *Forbes*, August 12, 1985.

Liquid Investments

The final category—liquid investments—presents far fewer choices in terms of sectors. Generally, the sector decision may be exactly the same as that reached on the previous level, namely, to keep a certain portion of the overall portfolio liquid by investing in a suitable money market fund. But some degree of differentiation is still possible.

You need to decide, for example, whether to place the assets you are targeting for liquidity in a general money market fund or in a government money market fund. During the early 1980s a series of uncertainties struck the higher levels of the American financial infrastructure. (I am referring to the collapse of the Penn Square Bank of Oklahoma City, the difficulties at the Continental Bank of Illinois, and the closing of the offices of a number of government bond dealers.) As a result, many investors began questioning the soundness of their money market investments, and opted for lower-yielding but safer money funds that invested only in U.S. Treasury and Agency instruments. More recently, a further classification has been added—the *prime money market fund.* In terms of safety, this type of fund falls somewhere between the government fund and the general fund. Its name refers to the fact that such a fund invests only in instruments of the highest quality ratings, whether issued by the government, banks, or corporations.

Thus you as an investor can choose among a number of different money market funds in making your investments. Your choice ought to reflect the "comfort level" you demand of your money market investments. But do not overlook the risk-reward parameters, as there is a definite trade-off between yield and safety. The lower the safety, the higher the yield will be. In fact, if you are an ambitious investor who would like to maximize yield at the expense of safety, even in the liquid investments sector, you have an alternative available to you. Over the last few years a number of new funds—*short-term bond funds*—have been launched. These funds do not qualify as money market funds because a considerable portion of their portfolios matures in more than a year. (A year is generally regarded as the line of demarcation for an instrument to be called a *cash equivalent investment.*) Some short-term bond funds have a maturity time of as low as one to one and a half years. As a result, some investors may find the excess yield these funds offer quite attractive if they are willing to absorb some additional risk. In this case an investor faces the risk of a capital loss; this is because instruments of more than a year's duration have to be "marked to the market" on a daily basis. An average spread in rates between general money market funds and short-term bonds might be anywhere from 1.5 to 2.5 percent.

As we can see, sector allocation is a refinement of asset allocation. Sector allocation allows us to provide additional detail to the design of a portfolio. It allows us to define which sectors of the investment market are to be represented in our final portfolio as well as the proportions for each of these sectors. The result is a conceptual framework of how we want our portfolio structured for the immediate future.

CHAPTER ELEVEN

Step Four: Mutual Fund Selection

Now we are at the final stage of multifund investing: Step Four of the investment pyramid described in Figure 8–1. This stage involves the selection of mutual funds for our portfolio. We can assume that we have created a well-balanced and fully detailed portfolio. Its framework is sound. If we have approached its construction in the right way, it has the necessary flexibility to withstand the pressures of a volatile, complex market environment. All that is left for us now to do is to apply the "bricks and mortar," that is, to carefully select our mutual funds.

THE TRADITIONAL APPROACH VERSUS MULTIFUND INVESTING

First of all, let us examine a number of critical issues about this final step. Keep in mind that even traditional managers can use the same four-step approach to portfolio construction. But at Step Four the traditionalists will have to do research on some 10,000 equity issues and the bonds and debentures of between 3,000 and 4,000 corporations. What a time-consuming task! As we saw earlier, the time constraint on such managers forces choices on them that are in the end not to the benefit of their clients because of the strain they undergo in performing both portfolio management and security research.

By contrast, when we substitute mutual funds for stocks and bonds, Step Four is not the most time-consuming task. In fact, it is perhaps the *least* time-consuming task of all! On the surface this statement may seem preposterous. (Later on in this book—after you have had a chance to read Chapters Twelve and Thirteen—you will understand how true this claim is.)

Let us be clear again as to what we are doing in a conceptual way: we are breaking down the traditional functions of the professional investor into two roles. The first role is that of the portfolio manager (or portfolio designer). Chapters Nine and Ten have spelled out the details of the tasks assigned to the portfolio manager. He or she must have a keen sensitivity to the investor's objectives as well as an ability to absorb all the factors that influence the investment markets. After assessing how these factors may have an impact on various sectors of the market in the months to come, the portfolio manager has to design a sound portfolio structure.

THE MUTUAL FUND MANAGER'S ROLE

Step Four, by contrast, is concerned with the second role, which is that of the mutual fund manager. He or she will carefully select stocks and bonds for the portfolio designed by the portfolio manager. People assigned to this role are not the same as those assigned to portfolio management. Instead, the mutual fund managers are full-time specialists who devote their entire energy solely to the selection of stocks and bonds. They cannot be distracted from this task by the chores of portfolio management.

Both sets of professions—the portfolio managers and the mutual fund managers—work in harmony with each other. The impact of the mutual fund managers on the portfolio is not accidental or subject to dramatic variability. Instead, their role is both well defined and limited. This is because the investment plan that has been created through asset allocation and sector allocation has a number of precise "slots." To complete the portfolio, these slots have to be filled. If a mutual fund can fill a particular slot, it will be selected. But even if a selection is made in error, and that fund fails to live up to expectations, its negative impact on the whole portfolio will be limited. For that particular fund fills only one slot in a multislotted portfolio.

Under multifund investing no single fund is allowed

to have an undue influence on the overall portfolio. No matter how bright a particular fund's prospects may appear at the moment, it would be foolhardy to believe that the fund will always continue to do so well in the future. Again, in multifund investing, we have no need to gamble on a specific fund, provided that we select all our funds according to the guidelines that will be described in detail in Chapters Twelve and Thirteen. The combination of a carefully selected group of funds will offer the consistent returns you and most other investors are seeking.

The crux, therefore, of multifund investing is a close coordination between two groups of investment professionals: portfolio managers and mutual fund managers. Each group performs a distinct role, but one group—the mutual fund managers—performs its role at the direction of the other group. In this coordination lie the orderliness and the symmetry of multifund investing.

WHAT ABOUT FEES?

For this reason, also, professional investors or fiduciaries who are implementing the multifund investing approach on behalf of clients should understand why there is no doubling or pyramiding of fees. A cursory glance at multifund investing might suggest that we have to deal here with an unnecessary layering of fees. Some uninitiated investors might believe that an extra layer of management—with all its concomitant costs—has been built into the process for no reason. Far from it! No layering has occurred without explanation. There are two separate sets of managers performing two distinct sets of functions. Each set must be remunerated for its respective role and functions.

I often respond to this charge with the following example. Let us suppose that, instead of placing their assets in stocks and bonds, investors had the opportunity to place them in a privately held corporation. Let us also assume that these investors wished to maintain a "silent" role—that of disinterested, passive partners. The first step would be to employ a qualified individual to fill the position of chief executive officer. That professional would be empowered to develop a strategy for the company, a business plan, flowcharts, and all the other tools by which management sets policy and direction for a business. The silent owners would be consulted periodically to ensure that management's strategy and philosophy were to their liking and reflected their goals for the company.

The investors, however, would not expect the chief executive officer to perform all of the various tasks of the day-to-day running of the company. Instead, we might reasonably expect that the chief executive officer would, in turn, hire a team of senior officers (and line managers, in the case of a manufacturing firm) to implement the strategy developed jointly with the investors. The role of the chief executive officer at that point would be to oversee operations, to ensure that the agreed-upon strategy was properly implemented, that directions were carried out according to specifications, and that the company was meeting its objectives.

Let us carry the analogy over to the multifund portfolio. The portfolio manager is the chief executive officer. In conjunction with the investor, that manager develops the objectives, or policy, of the investment portfolio. Next, the manager creates a strategy, or business plan. By this we mean the asset allocation and sector allocation by means of which the portfolio is to achieve its objectives. Finally, the manager hires a team of professionals—the mutual fund managers—to implement that investment plan on a day-to-day basis. Afterward, as we shall see later, the portfolio manager, or chief executive officer, oversees the junior officers to make sure that they are performing their assigned tasks. These tasks include the selection of emerging growth stocks, convertible bonds, and basic industrial stocks, among others. Periodically the chief executive officer or portfolio manager has to recheck the portfolio to make sure that it is fulfilling its expectations. This means that he or she reviews the portfolio's asset allocation and sector allocation.

What pyramiding of fees is there? The chief executive officer–portfolio manager must be paid, and the junior officers–mutual fund managers must be remunerated as well. If you accept the basic premise of this book—that the investment world today is too complex and fast-moving for one individual to wear two hats (that of portfolio manager and stock-and-bond selector)—there is no claim to be made for any supposed layering of undue expenses.

Let us look at this question from a different perspective. It is generally agreed that bank trust officers—out of all investment professionals—face a most restrictive set of covenants governing the procedures they must follow in order to invest their trusteed assets. The "legal list" concept as to which securities are fit investments for a trust account has only recently fallen by the wayside. Between national and state trust regulations, a fixed set of guidelines has been created to strictly govern trust investment procedures. Yet, as mentioned in Chapter Five, the comptroller of the currency has ruled that mutual funds are an absolutely suitable investment for trust accounts. He found no impropriety in the fact that a trust account invested in mutual funds would indirectly incur a second set of fees (beyond the trustee fees charged by the bank itself). In itself, Trust Circular 4 should be all the proof anyone needs that the multifund investing approach does not involve any unnecessary fees or expenses.

A DIVERSITY OF FUNDS

One further point: As we begin to describe the process of selecting mutual funds for the portfolio, it is important to keep in mind the extent to which we will utilize these funds. We have defined five primary sectors in the portfo-lio's framework: aggressive growth, conservative growth, equity-income, fixed-income, and money market. Can we infer from that structure that a portfolio will consist of no more than five funds? Absolutely not!

When we speak of multifund investing, we are talking of portfolios consisting of perhaps 10 to 20 funds in all. Each sector in itself will be a multifund portfolio. We will not have one aggressive growth fund, but three, four, or five aggressive growth funds. Not one fixed-income fund, but three, four, or five bond funds. Each one will be selected for a specific strength or area of expertise it can bring to the overall portfolio. As we shall examine in greater depth later, this multistyle structuring of the investments is a critical ingredient in the reduction of risk and the smoothing out of the performance curve.

PERFORMANCE AS A VARIABLE

Performance is the least dependable variable in multi-fund investing. (This is a point that will be discussed further in Chapters Twelve and Thirteen.) A great num-ber of studies of the performance of investment managers have concluded that the correlation between one year's performance and that of the next year is horrendously low. For example, a study conducted by the Becker Funds Evaluation Service (now the SEI Funds Evaluation) re-vealed that 80 percent of the equity managers ranked in the top half of all managers one year were ranked in the bottom half the following year. Another study by the same organization found that less than 1 percent of man-agers surveyed over an eight-year period (1974–81) ranked in the top quartile for all eight years. Only after the criterion was reduced to ranking in the top quartile in only two out of the eight years did more than 50 percent of these managers qualify.

In view of this schizophrenic record, you will understand why we suggested earlier that no one fund should represent an unduly large proportion of your total asset base. Mutual fund managers are as subject to the variabilities of performance as the private account managers surveyed by Becker. While we shall attempt to screen out funds with the widest variations in performance from year to year, we still have no guarantee that the remaining candidates can offer any greater assurance as to their future performance.

This is the crucial aspect of true multifund investing. No one fund, no one asset class, and no one sector can guarantee us success. We will, therefore, always fully diversify our portfolios by asset classes, by sectors, and by styles of funds within sectors.

CHAPTER TWELVE

The Wrong Way to
Mutual Fund Selection

Multifund investing can be compared to a two-pronged instrument. On the first prong we have to put together our portfolio plan, or framework. Using the first three steps of Figure 8–1, we set our objective, and then we did our asset allocation and sector allocation. Now we have come to the second prong—the point at which we have to carry out the task of selecting mutual funds for our portfolio. When all these tasks are completed, the two prongs of the investing process will converge. We shall then have a fully described portfolio.

How can we detail all the steps involved in correctly selecting mutual funds for our portfolio? Surprisingly enough, the best way to describe this process is to begin by telling you how *not* to select funds. As the number of funds available to us continues to grow, and as more and more attention is paid to the entire mutual fund industry, our chances of making a mistake increase commensurately.

TRAP NO. 1: THE LATEST RAGE

An uninformed investor is prone to fall into a great many traps. The most obvious of these pitfalls is to ask ourselves, "What fund is hot right now?" It's only normal for an unskilled mutual fund investor to be enticed by the latest rage. This is hardly a new phenomenon. In the late 1960s we had the "onics craze," when apparently every new stock issue had *onics* tacked onto the end of its name. Naturally many funds launched at that time concentrated their portfolios on such stocks; they were the fastest-growing funds of those years. In the early 70s we had portfolio managers known as the "gunslingers" or "Young Turks." They scrapped the old style of prudent investment and in its place developed an aggressive approach to investing. Sure enough, a rash of "go-go" funds soon emerged, attracting what for those days was an astronomical sum of money. (Can anyone forget the ill-fated launch of the Manhattan Fund? Jerry Tsai, a noted go-go fund manager at the Fidelity group of Boston, left to start his own organization. Manhattan Fund was launched based on his reputation, raised hundreds of millions of dollars on the offering, but failed to live up to expectations.) In early 1983 we saw the launch of numerous high-tech funds, as the craze for technology stocks reached its peak. This craze was fueled by the astronomical gains such stocks had enjoyed since the onset of the bull market in August 1982. Currently government securities funds are all the rage. It seems the mutual fund industry is always wise enough to have products available for what is "hot" right now.

Unfortunately for the novice, as the *Business Week* article cited on page 135 ("Why 'Specialty' Funds Are Risky Business") correctly noted, investment themes become hottest at their peak. The rush of money from the masses comes at absolutely the worst time. Onics stocks began to decline when sales of those funds were at their height. The great bear market of 1973–74 followed closely on the heels of the boom in go-go funds. Technology stocks went into a prolonged eclipse shortly after the launch of most high-tech funds. It happens time and again, but uninitiated investors always come back for more punishment.

That is why we pointed out in Chapter Ten that, in setting their objectives, successful investors should keep their sights firmly focused on their objectives and not be swayed by current fads or crazes. The returns from "hot" funds are always alluring, but they are illusory in the sense that they are not long-lasting. Like a nova, they are very bright for a while, but then quickly disappear.

TRAP NO. 2:
THE CULT OF PERFORMANCE

In addition to funds that are hot because of current vogue, another trap waits for unsuspecting mutual fund investors—the cult of performance. Many investors fall prey to last year's top-performing funds. It appears quite logical to invest in funds that are currently superperformers. Isn't it reasonable to assume that a fund providing superior performance will continue to do so for an extended period of time? Unfortunately, such is not the case. Too often yesterday's superperformer is today's subpar performer, as Table 12–1 clearly shows.

A number of observations are in order about Table 12–1. First, there is clearly no correlation between a fund's ranking one year and the ranking it attains the following year. Keep in mind that if you purchase a fund that has performed well one year, you have no guarantee at all that it will turn in a superior performance in the future. In fact, you have no guarantee that its performance will be even average! There is no consistency or pattern at all to these rankings. A fund ranked in the top 10 one year has an equal chance of appearing either in the top or bottom half the following year, or the year after. Nor does it seem to matter whether the fund achieved this ranking in a rising market, a flat market, or a declining market. No matter what the market environment was the following year, there was no correlation in the fund's performance. In fact, an examination of the trends from the mid-70s to the mid-80s seems to indicate a far more pronounced decline in the most recent years.

Second, the top 10 list is often dominated by a single investment theme. For instance, the top 10 list for 1983 was heavily weighted with funds whose portfolios concen-

TABLE 12–1 Top 10 Funds (1975–1984)

Top in 1975	1976 Rank	1977 Rank	Top in 1976	1977 Rank	1978 Rank
44 Wall Street	21	33	Sequoia	23	28
Putnam Capital	2	385	Putnam Capital	385	362
Penn Mutual	15	16	Gemini	130	406
Gemini	3	130	Acorn	28	77
P/C Capital	31	393	Twentieth Century Growth	45	3
Leverage Fund of Boston	7	340	Pioneer II	17	99
Oppenheimer Special	14	15	Leverage Fund of Boston	340	94
Sigma Venture	175	4	Safeco Growth	35	70
American Capital Venture	164	10	Mutual Shares	37	69
Scudder Development	203	12	Security Ultra	165	31

Top in 1977	1978 Rank	1979 Rank	Top in 1978	1979 Rank	1980 Rank
Value Line Leverage Growth	18	176	Merrill Lynch Pacific	434	106
United Services Gold	247	2	GT Pacific	435	130
Strategic Investments	140	1	Twentieth Century Growth	8	9
Sigma Venture	42	94	Evergreen	40	55
International Investors	168	3	Twentieth Century Select	38	56
Franklin Gold	173	4	Lord Abbett Developing Growth	131	129
Lindner Fund	35	147	National Aviation & Technology	254	196
American Capital Pace	32	43	44 Wall Street	9	122
Explorer Fund	53	100	Charter	48	151
American Capital Venture	27	36	American Capital Growth	13	19

Top in 1979

Top in 1979	1980 Rank	1981 Rank
Strategic Investments	8	469
United Services Gold	4	470
International Investors	18	462
Franklin Gold	14	452
Keystone Precious Metals	27	466
Golconda Investors	80	456
Constellation Growth	7	454
Twentieth Century Growth	9	360
44 Wall Street	121	492
Quasar Associates	29	353

Top in 1980

Top in 1980	1981 Rank	1982 Rank
Hemisphere	430	56
Nautilus	265	97
Hartwell Leverage	437	211
United Services Gold	470	4
Stein Roe Capital	450	292
IDS Growth	98	125
Constellation Growth	454	426
Strategic Investments	469	5
Twentieth Century Growth	360	468
American Capital Enterprise	433	395

Top in 1981

Top in 1981	1982 Rank	1983 Rank
Oppenheimer Target	1	140
Lindner Fund	255	138
Quest for Value	42	17
Lindner Dividend	169	7
Vanguard Quality I	91	41
Mutual Qualified Income	420	31
Merrill Lynch Pacific	492	20
Sequoia	157	90
Franklin Utilities	149	310
Delta Trend	164	21

Top in 1982

Top in 1982	1983 Rank	1984 Rank
Oppenheimer Target	140	603
Loomis-Sayles Capital	317	525
NEL Growth	416	502
United Services Gold	553	636
Strategic Investments	562	641
IDS Progressive	272	460
Fidelity Select Technology	3	599
Putnam Vista	329	550
Mass. Financial Growth	55	510
Fidelity Select Precious Metals	550	629

TABLE 12–1 (concluded)

Top in 1983	1984 Rank	1985 Rank	Top in 1984	1985 Rank
DIT Aggressive Growth	418	34	Prudential Bache Utility	117
Oppenheimer Regency	620	159	Vanguard Qualified I	207
Fidelity Select Technology	599	740	Copley Tax Managed	387
Alliance Technology	598	341	American Telecommunication Income	122
First Investors Discovery	639	684	Franklin Utilities	462
Strong Investment	175	582	Stratton Monthly Division	212
Lindner Dividend	34	635	Fidelity Select Utilities	157
Royce Value	378	287	Fidelity Qualified Dividend	368
Legg Mason Value	86	155	Windsor Fund	268
Hemisphere	499	8	Sequoia	274

SOURCE: Lipper Analytical Services.

trated on technology. When technology fell out of vogue the following year, one could easily predict what would happen to the funds that were the 1983 stars. Or let us examine 1979's list, which was dominated by funds investing in gold and gold stocks. Within two years the rankings of those funds collapsed. It almost amounts to a new theme per year!

Since investment themes come and go, there is no way to predict when a particular theme will come into ascendancy. Once it has risen to the heights, there is no way to predict how long it will remain in favor. We need to recall that the period to observe is no longer from year to year but from quarter to quarter. As we pointed out in Chapter One, volatility seems to be creating ever shorter periods both in terms of overall market movements and the performance of individual sectors of the market. Therefore, if you invest in last year's leading funds in the hope of providing a "comfort level" for yourself, you may achieve just the opposite result.

Why does this happen so often? Why do funds ranked high one year have a difficult time maintaining their relative rank? Shifts in investment themes explain part of the phenomenon. The rest can be related to portfolio structuring, such as a tacit decision by the portfolio manager to adopt an extremely restricted viewpoint. Mutual funds can establish a broadly based approach by spreading their assets across the full spectrum of equity and/or debt instruments. (It's worthwhile to note, for instance, that few of the top funds for 1983 and 1984 had broadly based portfolios.) Or mutual funds can concentrate on either one niche or only a few niches. As themes rise and fall in popularity, the limited-sphere funds fortunate enough to have their portfolios focused on a popular theme will stand out accordingly. For example, a fund whose portfolio had over 50 percent of its assets in technology stocks in 1983, as many did, of necessity outperformed a fund whose portfolio was spread across many themes and had only 10 percent in the technology area. But quite obviously, the leverage works in the opposite direction when a particular theme like technology passes its peak.

This particular trap—the cult of performance—is reinforced by what we read in the press. Unfortunately, most investors look to the press as their primary source of information. Which fund managers are interviewed in industry overviews or in year-end reviews? That year's top 10 performers, of course. Which fund managers are termed brilliant and given accolades—average performers or superior performers? Occasionally the focus may shift to managers who have accumulated a respectable long-term performance, but rarely are the average annual returns of those managers' funds as dramatic as the rate of a fund that rose 30 to 40 percent in a single year. Many sociologists call our current era the "age of instant gratification." The same development seems to be occurring in the world of mutual funds. The average investor is prone to say, "Don't tell me what's been doing fairly well in recent years. Tell me what's hot right now." What a fatal mistake!

Let us put to rest the cult of performance with one parting shot. As the attractiveness of mutual funds grows, so, too, does the number of advisory letters about the funds. If you read such publications because of a growing interest in such funds, ask yourself the following questions: Upon what do the authors of these letters base their predictions? Have they interviewed the portfolio manager in question? Do they have a clear sense of the investment strategy followed at that fund? Do they know how long the current portfolio manager has been at the helm? Do they know if the fund is run by an individual or by a committee? Or, rather, are recommendations in the advisory letters predicated solely or primarily on past performance? Mutual funds are required to place the following disclaimer in their advertising: "Past performance is no guarantee of future performance." Mutual fund advisory letters should be required to carry the same warning.

TRAP NO. 3: RANDOM SELECTION

Yet another trap awaits the novice investor: the practice of random selection. It is natural for such an investor to believe that since mutual funds in general perform well, a random selection of funds might provide satisfactory results. This assumption would be true if there were a narrow range of performance between the funds with the best results and those with the worst results. Unfortunately, as Table 12–2 reveals, the range is dramatically wide. If you could be assured of buying an "average fund," everything would be fine. But the dangers of purchasing underperforming funds mitigate against the practice of random selection.

AN ALTERNATIVE APPROACH: THE LONG–TERM SUPERIOR PERFORMERS

Let us give up, then, the concept of random selection and seek a remedy to our problem in an entirely different direction. Instead of looking for candidates for our portfolio among the superior performing mutual funds of a particular year, let us seek out the funds that have turned in a fine performance for an extended period. (This approach will lay the groundwork for the discussion in the following chapter, which takes up the right way to select mutual funds.) The best way to our alternative approach is to study Table 12–3, which lists the 10 top-performing

TABLE 12–2 Top-Performing and Bottom-Performing Mutual Funds (1975–1984)

Year	Top-Performing Funds	Return	Bottom-Performing Funds	Return
1975	44 Wall Street	+ 184.1%	United Services	− 38.3%
1976	Sequoia	+ 72.5	Strategic Investments	− 48.7
1977	Value Line Leverage Growth	+ 51.5	Chandler Fund	− 24.5
1978	Merrill Lynch Pacific	+ 59.2	Bear Fund	− 32.7
1979	Strategic Investments	+ 194.6	Bear Fund	− 31.6
1980	Hemisphere	+ 171.7	Kaufmann Fund	− 27.6
1981	Oppenheimer Target	+ 48.2	Bascom Hill Investments	− 56.2
1982	Oppenheimer Target	+ 81.3	Directors Capital	− 58.0
1983	DIT Aggressive Growth	+ 58.7	GSC Performance	− 19.4
1984	Prudential Bache Utility	+ 38.6	44 Wall Street	− 59.6

SOURCE: Lipper Analytical Services.

TABLE 12–3 Top 10 Mutual Funds over a 10-Year Period (1974–83)

Mutual Funds	Year-by-Year Ranking									
	1983	1982	1981	1980	1979	1978	1977	1976	1975	1974
Fidelity Magellan	17	16	19	14	26	10	40	47	—	—
Penn Mutual	11	116	254	248	89	86	17	14	2	521
Lindner Fund	134	260	2	165	156	33	8	10	61	—
Evergreen	55	381	310	54	40	4	12	15	14	—
Twentieth Century Growth	137	484	378	7	8	3	44	5	63	412
Twentieth Century Select	56	34	247	55	38	5	15	34	22	393
American Capital Venture	341	15	30	211	36	25	11	189	5	—
Sequoia	86	158	8	364	351	26	23	2	12	—
Oppenheimer Special	79	358	376	60	53	42	16	13	3	140
American Capital Pace	229	14	21	63	44	30	9	151	166	125

SOURCE: Lipper Analytical Services.

funds over a 10-year period. As we examine the record of the long-term top-performing funds, let us look for some corollary among their year-by-year performances.

Is there such a corollary? The answer is a resounding no! If you tried to identify these long-term top-performing funds by their appearance in a single year's top 10 ranking, you would have a difficult time indeed. *Long-term superior performers rarely provide superior performance in any single year.* Let us now sum up our findings: Successful multifund investing is not predicated on investing in one-year winners. Successful mutual fund selection is not based on what is the latest rage, nor on random selection.

The Right Way to
Mutual Fund Selection

Table 12–3 at the close of the previous chapter holds the key to correct multifund investing. *Success does not come by investing in one-year superior performers, but by identifying consistent, above average performers.* What we are looking for are funds with a well-defined investment philosophy which when implemented over an extended time frame have resulted in the delivery to investors of satisfactory returns. The screening process for such funds is twofold.

TWO KEY CONCEPTS

The two key words in the above paragraph are *above average* and *consistent.* They spell the differences between correctly and incorrectly selecting mutual funds. By above average, we simply mean funds that consistently rank in the top half of all available funds. We are not talking about the top 10 performers but about funds in the top 50 percent. Our parameters are so broad because, within the universe of mutual funds, there is possibly the greatest accumulation of investment talent today. As a group, therefore, they should generally perform as well as or better than broad stock and bond market barometers. If so, limiting one's investment to the top 50 percent of that group will provide a high degree of assurance that our portfolio of funds will turn in above average performance.

On the surface, this may appear to be too broad a parameter, but we will shortly show its correctness. For now, consider the sharp divergence in year-to-year performance returns provided by most investment managers (as shown in Table 12–2 on page 164). All a fund has to do to achieve top ranking for the long term is stay above the 50th percentile on a year-to-year basis. On the other hand, portfolio managers who rank in the top decile one year, bottom quartile the next, second quartile the following, seventh decile in the fourth year, and top quartile the fifth will find it virtually impossible to come out ahead of the manager who ranked in the first or second quartiles consistently. As we saw in Table 12–3 on page 165 regarding the top 10 funds for 10 years, the important thing is to achieve a good, or above average, performance—not a spectacular one.

Consistency is the second key concept. There are a number of reasons for seeking consistency, most pertaining to the psychological aspects of investing. Consider, for instance, two hypothetical funds. Both have appreciated 60 percent over a three-year time period, but by following quite different courses. Fund A rose 45 percent in value the first year, declined 5 percent the second year, and appreciated 16 percent in the third year. Fund B rose 25 percent in value the first year, 15 percent the second, and 11 percent the third. True, both Funds A & B have now appreciated 60 percent, but which one provided a higher "comfort level"? In view of the ever-present fear of shocks which exists in the investment world today, we have to ascribe some value to the mental ease provided by the steady performance of an investment. Compare the stability of Fund B to the "roller coaster" queasiness we might get from an investment such as Fund A.

There is another psychological aspect of seeking to invest in consistent funds. As we saw in Chapter Twelve, we need to avoid the trap of looking for the latest rage in funds. Even if we were to discover the Fund A of the mutual fund universe, finding it would turn out to be (a) a futile exercise, and (b) no guarantee of future performance. Thus even if an above average fund were able to provide the same results as a more consistent fund, we would still not gain anything. This is because we do not intend to have any single fund as the sole holding or a significant portion of our portfolio, which would normally consist of 10 to 20 funds. Even one or two spectacular yearly performances in a five-year period would not have a dramatic effect on the performance of our total portfolio. We might expect, for example, that the years in which the superperforming funds were at the peak of their performance curve would correspond with good years for other above average funds. So the total effect on our portfolio's performance would be marginal in good years.

On the other hand, such a fund can have a markedly detrimental effect in a year when it has a poor performance. Let us assume, for instance, that nine funds in our portfolio rank slightly above the median in a given year, while the 10th fund—one of these wild gyrators—is at the very bottom of its performance curve. As a result, our total portfolio would fail to achieve a fair record for that year. Because of the performance of that 10th fund, the total portfolio would have a subpar year. As you can see, there is nothing to be gained by including that fund in the portfolio—and much to lose.

Those who invest on behalf of others are confronted by yet another consideration of a psychological nature: What kind of performance figures do they wish to report to their clients? Speaking from personal experience, I have found that reporting consistent but not spectacular performance year-in and year-out is an "easy sell." It's true that such a fiduciary will probably never have "bragging rights" over a dramatic year with a performance record of plus 40 or plus 50 percent. But then again, he or she will never have to fear to answer the phone when the year's results are minus 30 or minus 40 percent!

This problem brings us to a misconception most financial counselors have about their clients. Typical clients are content with returns of between 15 and 20 percent. They do not expect returns of 30 to 40 percent per year, because they know that such a level is unattainable on a regular basis through financial investments. If people—by reason of their temperament—want annual returns of

30 to 40 percent, they will invest in venture capital, raw land, or some other kind of high-risk undertaking. They will not be in the stock and bond market. Clients respect consistent returns of a credible nature far more than they do wildly gyrating returns. Financial advisers who achieve gains year after year—even though these gains may be small in marginal years—have accomplished something. It is much better to have that kind of record than to expose one's clients to the wild ups and downs that the market as a whole has experienced in recent years.

Up until now we have been talking about the psychological advantages of consistency in investing. Let us discuss next the statistical aspects of this issue. If your goal is to achieve a certain long-term objective, are you not more likely to do so through consistent returns rather than through wildly gyrating investments with returns ranging from the spectacular to the subpar? Why is this so? *It's because every time you experience a loss, you now have two goals to achieve: (a) to make up the loss, and (b) to achieve your original objective!* Even though this concept is basic, many investors—both individuals and professionals—apparently overlook it. Losses are abominable not only because they shrink the capital base but also because they confront investors with these two tasks.

As we reported in Chapter Twelve, investors who were trapped by the go-go funds of the early 1970s or the high-tech funds of the early 80s were placed at a tremendous disadvantage. It has taken over 12 years and two bull markets to pull investors of the early 70s in those go-go funds back to where they started. If we factor in the costs of lost opportunities and inflation, those investors are still far behind where they should be. The more recent investors in high-tech funds might have an equally lengthy and arduous road ahead of them.

This point is not theoretical; it is pure mathematics. To prove it, let us consider another hypothetical mutual fund. According to its performance record, Fund C has risen in value by as much as 40 percent in a single year out of the past five years. It has also declined by 30 percent in a single year. If this appears to be an absurd example, we need only review the one-year turnaround in performance of some of 1983's top 10 funds cited in Table 12–1 on page 158. The pattern traced by those 1983 funds was very like that of our hypothetical Fund C. Investors enjoy seeing their investment rise in value by 40 percent in a single year. But what if in the year following your investment Fund C should decline by 30 percent? Now Fund C would have to appreciate by 43 percent just to get back to its original starting point (100 minus 30 percent equals 70; 70 times 142.86 percent equals 100). The situation would be even worse if we assume that these investors' five-year objective was to have their capital grow by 15 percent per year. This means that Fund C would have to appreciate by 287 percent in the remaining four years if the investors are to reach their objective. (100 times 15 percent times 5 years equals 201.14; 201.14 divided by 70 equals 287.34 percent.) If we assume that Fund C is a load fund with an initial sales charge of 8.5 percent, the rebound would have to be even greater if the investors are to break even or to achieve their initial objective.

This is the statistical trap that faces investors in funds with widely divergent patterns of performance. They would be comforted if their investment was worth 140 percent of its initial value after only a year. Even a subsequent decline of 30 percent could be weathered. But because of the statistical probabilities, no one can forecast which will come first—the plus 40 percent or the minus 30 percent. No asset allocation model or computer simulation can project with any assurance whether future patterns of performance will match the patterns of the past. Neither is there any way to predict the order in which the experience of past years would reoccur. In other words, there is absolutely no way to predict whether next year's performance will be minus 30 percent or plus 40 percent.

By way of contrast, a consistent fund never places investors in such a bind. Pluses, or at worst small losses, are linked to pluses. It is almost immaterial how large or small those pluses are, as long as they occur. The fact that a fund is above average as well as consistent provides us as investors with the implicit "insurance policy" we need to achieve our objectives. A consistent but below average fund achieves nothing. But a fund that is both consistent and above average is like a double-powered weapon. When carefully handled (as we will see later), such a fund is virtually unstoppable.

Our task is to identify funds with a consistent, above average performance whose managers have a sound investment philosophy. As we said at the beginning of this chapter, this involves a two-part screening process. Remember that we are dealing with a universe of over 1,300 stock and bond mutual funds. We have to reduce this total to as manageable a number as possible before beginning the more intensive part of the screening. Otherwise we will be in virtually the same bind as the one that confronts stock and bond analysts. Our aim is to make Step Four—mutual fund selection—the least time-consuming aspect of investing.

EXAMINING THE HISTORICAL DATA

The first part of the screening process reduces perceptibly the list of candidates. In fact, it rules out over 90 percent of the universe of mutual funds! We begin by examining the historical data on all available funds to find those that have provided consistent, above average returns. At a minimum we will look at records for a period of three years; a five-year period would be preferable. But beyond a period of five years it is difficult to assess the value of the data. This is because we need to take into account the rapid changes that have taken place in the market environment, philosophies of investment, and portfolio managers.

Keep in mind also that we have to review the year-by-year performance of the funds, not their cumulative returns. If you recall the hypothetical returns for Funds A and B mentioned earlier in this chapter, you will understand the reason for this procedure. Cumulative returns—whether for a period of 3, 5, or 10 years—do not allow us to measure for consistency of performance. And consistency is one of the key ingredients we are seeking. Of course, this is a bit more work than just scanning a list of top-performing funds for the past three or five years. But this extra trouble will keep us from falling into the pitfall of considering only cumulative returns. Besides, investors have available a number of statistical sources, such as Lipper Analytical Services, Inc., Wiesenberger Investment Services, and CDA Investment Technologies. Some of these services are available for more sophisticated individual investors through on-line databases. As a result, such a detailed historical analysis is not difficult or time-consuming.

There are a number of ways to carry out this analysis. Funds can be measured against their peers (for example, aggressive growth funds versus other aggressive growth funds; high-yield bond funds versus other high-yield bond funds). We can also measure funds against broader subsets (for example, equity funds versus other equity funds, or bond funds versus other bond funds) as well as against the entire universe of mutual funds. Which parameters you use and the number of years you analyze will determine how many funds make it through this first screening. My personal experience over the past 10 years and more has been that no more than 70 to 80 candidates will qualify for your consideration. That amounts to *less than 6 percent* of the currently available 1,300 open-ended stock and bond funds. You are beginning to see why we claim that mutual fund selection can be the least time-consuming step in the investment pyramid. Although we are only halfway through the screening process, our list of candidates has shrunk to no more than 70 or 80 funds.

For safety's sake you should analyze the data on performance from a number of perspectives; one screening is not enough. If you as a potential investor had used as your test base the period 1979–1981—a time of generally rising interest rates—and if you had measured funds only against the total universe of funds, no bond funds at all would have made it through your screening. Let us carry this forward in time to early 1982 when you would be going through the four-step process of creating your portfolio. Your asset allocation and sector allocation—Steps Two and Three in multifund investing—would call for investing a significant portion of your assets in bond funds (on the basis of a projection of lower interest rates in the future). Yet you would not have any candidates to fill the slots allocated for bond funds. You can see, therefore, how important it is for you to compare peer funds with peer funds as well as to examine the total range of funds.

Now that we have completed the statistical screening process, we are halfway done. But we cannot take any shortcut by stopping here. Even though we have identified a list of funds with a consistent, above average performance record, these funds have qualified only on the basis of their past performance. But we all know that past performance is no guarantee of what will happen in the future. So we must take our screening one step further to personalization.

THE PERSONALIZATION TEST

The *personalization* test is a method by which we acquire information on how the management of a mutual fund operates. Why do we need information of this kind? Why can we not simply rely on the data about the fund's past performance? An article by Karen Slater in the December 30, 1985 issue of *The Wall Street Journal* provides a perfect answer to such questions. After pointing out that the 44 Wall Street Fund was ranked by Lipper Analytical Services, Inc. as the first out of 421 funds for the five-year period ending in 1979, the article discussed that fund's more recent performance:

> For the five years ended September 30, 1985, 44 Wall Street Fund was the worst-performing of 464 funds, says Lipper. . . . Like the "newer" funds proliferating today, Mr. Baker [the fund's portfolio manager] concentrates his investment in only a couple of industries. . . . On top of that, Mr. Baker is partial to volatile stocks and to troubled issues with turnaround potential. And he magnifies his task by holding as few as 10 stocks at a time and by investing borrowed money for added leverage.[1]

That sort of information comes from the personalization factor, not from reviewing data on a fund's historical performance. Did the data on past performance at the beginning of 1980 give any forewarning of what was to ensue? No, but a close investigation of the portfolio manager's rather unique investment style might have done so.

That is the essence of personalization—the process of going beyond mere performance data and bringing a fund candidate to "life" in the investor's mind. This process is

---

[1] Karen Slater, "Stellar Results Can Reverse Fast When Mutual Funds Stress Risks," *The Wall Street Journal,* December 30, 1985.

much like the traditional fundamental research procedure performed before one invests in the equity or debt issues of a corporation. In this case, however, we are researching the way a mutual fund's management operates.

A critic might ask whether, in addition to reviewing the data or figures on a fund's past performance, we only need to know its investment objective. The answer is no; that is not sufficient information for our purposes. After all, a firm's stated objective is simply the fund's "end" or goal. What our research has to tell us is the means that the fund's manager will take to achieve that end.

The example cited above—44 Wall Street—would be classified as an aggressive growth fund. But from that information alone we could not have realized that the fund was investing in a limited number of issues, many of which were in a turnaround situation. Neither did it tell us that leverage was used. The term *aggressive growth funds* is a broad umbrella under which many investment styles can fall, including small capitalization stocks, emerging growth companies, turnaround situations, deep cyclical stocks, high-technology issues, over-the-counter stocks, and new issues. We might well ask, "What's in a name?" Just to determine a mutual fund's classification does not give us a clear understanding of that fund's investment strategy. As proof of this statement, I might point out that many aggressive growth funds besides 44 Wall Street performed quite admirably after 1980. This particular fund did not.

Let us go one step further. Granted that neither the numbers (or figures) on a fund's past performance nor its stated objective are enough to give us a clear picture of a particular fund, can we rely on the fund's prospectus to supply the information we need? The answer, unfortunately, is no. Despite the good points of a prospectus, as we pointed out in Chapter Five, this document has certain limitations. The prospectuses of most mutual funds, for example, do not supply the information we need to "personalize" the management. Potential customers cannot learn from a prospectus who the day-to-day decision maker is. You will find a list of the fund's officers and directors, but you will not know that the real portfolio manager is some unnamed individual who reports to the officers and directors. You also will not learn how long the current decision maker has been in charge of the fund. An October 1985 article by John Heins in *Forbes* magazine pointed out:

> They [the clients] had no idea that the man who had been regularly beating the averages for them was gone. No announcement was made. . . . Two years ago the SEC put out for comment a proposal to request that the prospectus identify the portfolio manager, but it met such strong opposition from the industry that it was never adopted.[2]

There is another shortcoming to the prospectuses of many mutual funds: the intentionally vague language used to describe the investment objective or philosophy of the funds. Here, for example, is a passage from the prospectus of the New York Venture Fund, an aggressive growth fund:

> Our investment objective is growth of capital, although there is no assurance that we will succeed. We ordinarily invest in securities which our management believes have above-average appreciation potential. Usually these securities are common stocks. They may also be securities having some of the investment characteristics of common

[2] John Heins, "In the Dark," *Forbes,* October 21, 1985.

stocks, such as securities convertible into common stocks. Income is not a significant factor in selecting our investments.

Another aggressive growth fund, the Security Ultra Fund, makes this statement in one of its prospectuses:

The Fund's primary objective is to seek capital appreciation and emphasis is placed upon the selection of those securities which, in the opinion of the Investment Manager, offer the greatest potential for appreciation. . . . The Fund will ordinarily invest in a broadly diversified portfolio of common stocks and securities convertible into common stocks, although it reserves the right to invest in fixed income securities.

And here is a statement from the American Investors Income Fund, a bond fund with a quite unique investment style:

The objective of the Fund is income through the receipt of interest and dividends from a portfolio invested primarily in fixed-income securities and preferred stocks with comparatively generous yields, most of which will reflect speculative characteristics. A secondary objective of capital appreciation will be pursued to the limited extent that this objective is attainable from the foregoing investments, and through securities convertible into common stock.

Every rule has its exception, as does this one. Some funds are quite explicit in describing their investment methodology. But the examples provided above are more the norm than the exception. As a result, attempting to research a mutual fund through its prospectus can prove as unenlightening as researching a public company through its annual report. There is simply not enough hard data for you as a prospective investor to form an opinion.

What you do need to do, if at all possible, is to have a

face-to-face meeting with the principals of the fund so that you can gather information about the fund. If this is not practical, you should have contact by telephone with some qualified individual at the fund group who can transmit the information you need to know. Don't let yourself be shunted off to a so-called Shareholder Servicing Department. The type of information you require necessitates direct communication with someone in management—preferably the portfolio managers.

What sort of information do you need to know? First, you need to know about the corporate structure of the fund. Is its decision-making process handled by a committee or a "star system"? (Under the star system there is one key individual who is responsible for running the fund.) If we are dealing with a committee, we need to know whether it consists of the portfolio managers of the fund or funds, or of full-time investment analysts. If we are dealing with a star system, we need to know what the fund's record has been in retaining its key portfolio managers. Some major fund groups are notorious for their inability to retain key people.

We should also seek information about the security research process. Is there a qualified in-house analytic staff, or does the firm rely primarily on research provided by Wall Street sources? We need to obtain a more precise statement of the fund's investment philosophy and policies beyond that provided by the prospectus. Is there an investment credo that controls all subsequent investment decisions? Is the decision-making process rigid or free-form? I clearly recall one fund whose decision-making process was controlled by a precise, disciplined, computer-generated security screening process. The parameters were such that in early 1982 the computer's list of candidates was weighted heavily in favor of energy issues. All common sense at the time indicated that as a result of the decline in oil prices and demand, energy issues were definitely not the place to be investing. Yet this fund followed its discipline rigidly, and as a result its performance suffered greatly. In general, the inquiries at this stage of the screening process should communicate to us a good sense of what makes the management of that fund or fund group tick.

WHAT IS THE INVESTMENT STYLE?

The second stage of the personalized screening process is very critical because its questions have to do with the investment style of a fund or funds. What means are used in order to obtain the ends desired by the fund? Is this management style applied consistently, or does the fund allow some latitude for changing that management style in view of changes that may occur in the marketplace? Is the style broadly based so that it can capture a cross section of investment alternatives, or is it limited in scope (the way sector funds are limited)?

To clarify what is meant by this discussion, we might well consider the various investment styles of a few well-known funds. Mutual Shares, for example, devotes a substantial portion of its assets to companies whose balance sheets indicate strong values that—in the opinion of the portfolio managers—are not reflected in the market prices of those stocks or bonds. Such companies might include firms in receivership or under reorganization or subject to a takeover. Pennsylvania Mutual looks for stocks with a small capitalization and a strong cash flow per share. Pilgrim Magnacap applies to its security selection process precise parameters as to the relationship between a company's rising earnings and its rising dividends.

This type of information is perhaps the most critical of all because, as we shall see later, it is the final linchpin to success in multifund investing. We must be able to "tag" a fund, that is, to know what motivates it on a day-to-day basis and what area of expertise it brings to a multifund portfolio. We want to know how the investment style of that particular fund will complement the styles of other funds represented in the portfolio so as to have as little overlap or duplication as possible. One quick way to check for duplication is to look at the five largest portfolio holdings of a given fund. For example, I recently checked the five largest portfolio holdings of nine aggressive growth funds that had made it through my initial screening process. (This means checking out 45 different positions.) Not a single name appeared twice on my checklist! This is what I regard as the very essence of a properly performed style-identification.

To sum up, here is a checklist of the type of questions we need to ask in order to gather the information required in our personalization process:

1. Is the fund's decision-making process handled by a committee or a star system?
2. What is its record of retaining portfolio managers?
3. Is the research mainly done by in-house analysts or by outside sources?
4. What, precisely, is the investment philosophy or policy of the fund?
5. Is the decision-making process rigid or flexible?
6. What is the fund's investment style? What is its area of expertise?
7. Is its style broadly based or limited?
8. Is the style consistently applied, or does it change periodically?

After we have gone through the second stage of our screening process, we will find that the list of our candidate funds has shrunk even further. The personalization process will screen out certain funds with which we as investors are not comfortable for any number of reasons.

A particular fund may prove to have no depth of management; it may be a proverbial one-individual operation. Its performance record may be attributable to someone who is no longer with the fund. Its management style may be so abstruse that a potential investor cannot have a strong comfort level, as we reported was the case with the 44 Wall Street Fund. Perhaps the fund's investment style may be extremely similar to that of another fund that has made it through our screening process, or to that of another fund already in our portfolio. There are many reasons why funds may fail our personalization test.

What remains is a core group of mutual funds. No more than 30 to 35 funds may make it through both stages of the screening process. The surviving funds will become the "bricks and mortar" of our multifund portfolio. The framework is in place, and the proper "finishing materials" have been identified. We have finished the four-step process and reached the base of our investment pyramid. These are the mechanics of multifund investing. We have examined its theoretical and practical aspects.

We still have to analyze why multifund investing has proved so successful for many investors in many market environments and over such a long period. First, though, our next chapter will retrace the whole investing process again—this time in the form of a case study.

CHAPTER FOURTEEN

Creating a Multifund Portfolio

So far our discussion has focused on the theory of multifund investing. Let us now take all this information and build a real portfolio by applying the principles spelled out in the previous chapters. We will select a prototypical case, keeping in mind that the same process applies regardless of our objectives. We will follow the four-step process described in the investment pyramid (see Figure 8–1 on page 109).

The investors are a middle-aged couple who have enough money in savings to take care of emergencies. A separate savings account has been set up to pay for the projected college expenses of their two teenaged children. The couple own their own home, and their current mortgage payments represent a reasonable 25 percent of the annual family income. A benefits package provided by the husband's employer will take care of all contingency situations, such as major medical, disability, and dental expenses, as well as life insurance payments.

OBJECTIVE SETTING

The couple's assets available for investment, therefore, are primarily targeted for retirement planning. Both husband and wife are currently working, but would like to retire in approximately 10 to 15 years. By that time the children will have finished their schooling and be self-supporting. Additional savings accumulated over that period will supplement the current pool of capital for retirement purposes. In analyzing their situation by themselves or with the help of a financial counselor, the couple realize that their investment temperament is somewhat conservative. They are willing to devote some portion of their investable assets to growth-oriented investments, but in moderation. They would not be comfortable with any undue risk. In other words, they want to see their retirement nest egg grow as much as possible, but

FIGURE 14–1   Step One:
Objective Setting

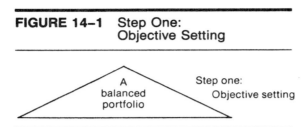

within reasonable bounds. The capital additions to the investment pool while both husband and wife are still working negate the necessity of sacrificing safety for the sake of accelerated growth (see Figure 14–1).

Such investors should adopt a balanced growth-and-income objective. This is a middle-of-the-road approach, not too conservative and not too aggressive. Equal emphasis should be placed on growth and income. The income is obviously not for current purposes. (In fact, we will invest all income as it is earned.) Indeed, the income will act as an anchor on the portfolio, muting risk and providing a measure of safety. This is because income-generating instruments, in general, are more risk-averse than growth vehicles. Such an objective seems to fit the investors' temperament.

ASSET ALLOCATION

Now that the objective has been determined—a balance between growth and income—we can turn our attention to Step Two: asset allocation. Looking at the factors that help us develop this allocation, we find that the economy is in a healthy state; it came out of a recession 12 months earlier. Prospects for sustained economic growth are favorable, and the Federal Reserve Board is maintaining a fairly reasonable stance on the growth of the money supply. Nor are there any indications of a forthcoming tightening of interest rates. These rates have been stable to slightly lower for some time, although according to the theory of the historic economic cycle, there should be some fear of higher rates in the next 9 to 15 months. At that point the recovery should be gaining additional momentum, thus placing a demand pressure on rates.

Nothing of particular significance is occurring on either the international or domestic political fronts. No tax or spending bills of any consequence are before Congress. The White House is not talking about new economic initiatives. Overall, we are left with a mildly optimistic scenario. Since this is a hypothetical example, we have simplified the fundamental analysis that has to be performed before creating an intelligent asset allocation. Our analysis is based on the assumptions that the investor follows the fundamentalist school and is not a technician.

Now let us take a look at the investment markets themselves. The stock market is in the midst of a prolonged advance that reflects the healthy state of the economy. This rally, with intermittent corrections, has had a fairly broad basis, and most market sectors have participated in it. On the fixed-income side, the bond market is also experiencing a significant rally, moving in line with the lower trend in interest rates. Recently, however, the bond rally has been faltering, as fears of a rebound in rates have surfaced.

This is the atmosphere in which we will create a balanced asset allocation. Since conditions for equity investment appear favorable, we will allocate 50 percent of the assets to growth investments. Until the upturn in rates is confirmed, we need not react prematurely. (We will keep in mind the liquidity of mutual funds and our ability to shift gears quickly if the need should arise.) Therefore, we will devote 45 percent of the assets to

---

FIGURE 14–2   Step Two: Asset Allocation

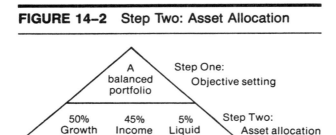

---

income investments. The remaining 5 percent will be kept liquid. This is a balanced asset allocation that places equal emphasis on growth and income (see Figure 14–2).

SECTOR ALLOCATION

Let us now proceed to the sector allocation. The short-term view of the environment presents an equally compelling argument in favor of both equity and debt investments. Accordingly, in our sector allocation for the 50 percent intended for growth, we will put 25 percent into aggressive-growth funds and 25 percent into conservative-growth funds. Although these investors are risk-averse, it is not unreasonable to have 25 percent of their portfolio in aggressive funds. If we were dealing here with investors with a growth or maximum growth objective, both the asset allocation and the sector allocation would be appreciably different. Assuming a similar economic and market environment, we would recommend putting perhaps 45 percent of the investment assets in aggressive-growth funds and 15 percent in conservative-growth funds for growth investors. But if they were maximum growth investors, we would recommend putting 60 percent into aggressive-growth funds and 20 percent into conservative-growth funds.

What about the 45 percent allocated for income-oriented investments? Inasmuch as we are attempting to maintain a balanced approach, the bulk of this allocation will go into fixed-income funds. However, since prospects for the equity market remain favorable, some allocation will be made to equity income, namely, 10 percent to equity-income funds and 35 percent to fixed-income funds. In turn, since our projections for the interest-rate environment remain positive, of the 35 percent targeted for fixed income, 25 percent will go into long-term funds (a mix of high-grade and lower-grade funds) and 10 percent into intermediate-term funds. That presumes a flat yield curve from the intermediate-term to the long-term. If there is an appreciable yield differential between the two, perhaps only 5 percent will be placed in intermediate-term bond funds.

As for the 5 percent targeted for liquid funds, let us assume that we are dealing with an environment without any scares in the financial system. In that case this 5 percent will go into a general money market fund. If our investors are "nervous," a prime or government-only fund can be used.

Finally, if our investors are in a high tax bracket, the 5 percent allocation to liquid might be placed in tax-free money market funds. (Please keep in mind the tax-conversion table in Chapter Ten.) This proposal also applies to the sector allocation for fixed income. Suitable tax-free bond funds can be substituted for taxable corporate bond funds. There is a broad array of choices available to us today in the universe of mutual funds: we can choose among a variety of long-term, short-term, high-grade, and low-grade tax-free funds.

A cursory overview of the suggested sector allocation might lead us to conclude that this portfolio is not balanced but rather tilted in favor of equities. As we can see in Figure 14–3, we plan to put 25 percent of the assets

FIGURE 14–3 Step Three: Sector Allocation

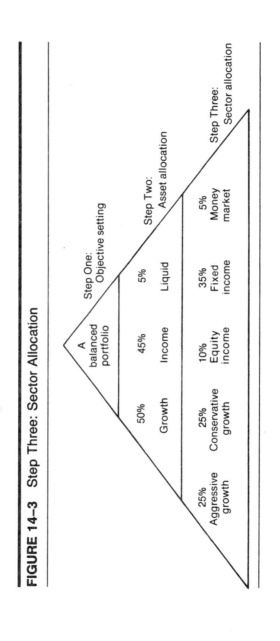

into aggressive-growth funds, 25 percent into conservative-growth funds, and 10 percent into equity-income
funds; this means a total of 60 percent of the portfolio
would be in equity-oriented funds. But this is not the case.
If we were to examine the underlying portfolios of each of
the aggressive-growth funds, conservative-growth funds,
and equity-income funds, we would find that some portion
of each fund's assets are invested in fixed-income or
money market instruments. Therefore, the portfolio is
truly balanced fairly evenly between growth vehicles and
income vehicles.

MUTUAL FUND SELECTION

We have now reached the final stage of multifund investing, when we select from our core group of mutual funds
to create the multifund portfolio. Keep in mind that we do
not want any single fund to have an undue influence on
the total portfolio. In addition, each sector has to be
invested in funds with a variety of investment styles so as
to provide further diversification of the portfolio.

There will be four funds in the aggressive-growth
sector. Fund A's style is to invest in emerging growth
stocks. Fund B invests in small capitalization stocks,
Fund C in deep cyclical issues, and Fund D in potential
turnaround situations. We will invest 6.25 percent of the
assets in each fund, for a total of 25 percent.

There will be three funds in the conservative-growth
sector. Fund E invests in companies with established
manufacturing (or service) lines, that is to say, in companies that are either industry leaders or among the top
three in a particular industry. Fund F invests in basic
value issues (issues with a lower price/earnings ratio and
a higher dividend rate than the Standard & Poor's 500
Stock Average). Fund G is a "stock picker," which means
that it does not have a preconceived bias toward any

particular industry, nor does it use financial screens. At the same time Fund G does not invest in more speculative issues. We will invest 8 percent of the assets in two of these funds, and 9 percent in the third fund. Since aggressive-growth funds bring more risk to the portfolio than conservative-growth funds, we have decided to use one more aggressive-growth fund than conservative-growth funds (even though on a percentage basis both groups have an equal weight in the portfolio).

We will use two funds in equity income. Fund H always keeps a preponderance of its portfolio in equities. Fund I will mix and match its portfolio between equity issues and debt issues, although there will be a slight bias toward equities. We will invest 5 percent of assets in each of these funds.

There will be four funds in the fixed-income sector. Fund J will be a long-term, high-grade bond fund. Fund K is a long-term, lower-grade bond fund. Fund L is a mixed-grade, mixed-maturity bond fund, while Fund M is an intermediate-term bond fund. In addition, all these funds are available in tax-free form for investors who can benefit from such an exclusion. We will invest 9 percent in Fund J, 8 percent in both Fund K and Fund L, and 10 percent in Fund M.

Finally, Fund N will be either a general market fund or a prime market fund. Alternatively, it may consist of a government-only money market fund. Figure 14–4 describes the mutual fund selection of this balanced portfolio. It also shows the completion of the investment pyramid.

* * *

The portfolio shown in Figure 14–4 is both a finished product and the quintessence of multifund investing. It is compact, streamlined, efficient, and totally flexible. It is

FIGURE 14–4 Step Four: Mutual Fund Selection—
the Completion of the Investment Pyramid

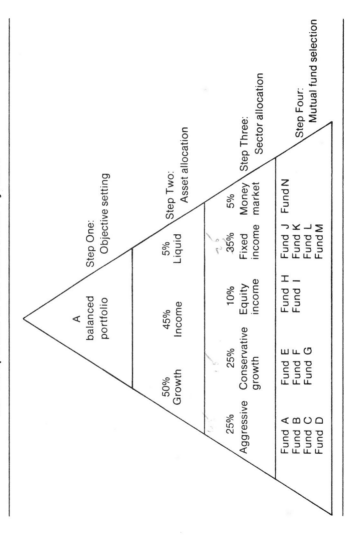

Step One:
Objective setting

A
balanced
portfolio

Step Two:
Asset allocation

50% Growth	45% Income	5% Liquid

Step Three:
Sector allocation

25% Aggressive	25% Conservative growth	10% Equity income	35% Fixed income	5% Money market

Step Four:
Mutual fund selection

Fund A	Fund E	Fund H	Fund J	Fund N
Fund B	Fund F	Fund I	Fund K	
Fund C	Fund G		Fund L	
Fund D			Fund M	

also easy to look after, as there are only 14 positions to monitor, not 30 to 40 stocks, 10 to 20 bonds, and 3 to 6 cash instruments. This portfolio has all the characteristics required to cope with a volatile, complex investment environment. And, of course, it is simple and straightforward to assemble either by part-time individual investors or full-time professionals.

Have we had to sacrifice anything in creating this new portfolio in terms of safety, prudence, or diversification? As we shall see in the next chapter, a multifund portfolio is the ultimate in risk-aversion and safety. Critics might believe—mistakenly—that there is safety in numbers, and that something has to be lacking in a portfolio with only 14 mutual funds. But if we total up the underlying stock, bond, and money market equivalents in these 14 funds, and if we keep in mind the care taken to prevent any duplication of investments, we will discover that this portfolio provides indirect ownership of *hundreds* of stocks, bonds, and money market instruments. As we pointed out in Chapter Six, a multifund portfolio offers both compactness and greater diversification.

What about the problem of complexity and the need of investors to shift certain stocks and bonds? We have here a portfolio of 14 themes, not one or two as in the traditional portfolio. Which type of portfolio is better equipped for today's complex marketplace? If any of these fourteen choices have to be changed, if the asset and/or sector allocations have to be adjusted, or if we modify objectives, we can do so with one or two phone calls. What is the reason for this flexibility? We are investing through mutual funds, the most liquid method of participating in the equity and debt markets.

CHAPTER FIFTEEN

The Triple Safety Net

Multifund investing has worked for an extended period of time in many different market environments and for investors with a wide array of goals and objectives. It has delivered consistent, above average returns while many other approaches to investment have floundered. What is the reason for this extraordinary record? What explains its consistency, its steadiness in the most turbulent conditions? Some previously enumerated features, such as compactness, efficiency, and flexibility, provide only part of the answer. A feature unique to multifund investing is the true explanation: *A multifund portfolio is diversified on three separate levels.*

It is an axiom of investing that the greater the diversification, the lower the risk. To repeat, if we invest all our assets in a single stock, we are at far greater risk than if we invest them in 10 stocks. If our assets are invested solely in equities, they are at far greater risk than if they were spread across a variety of stocks, bonds, and money market instruments. If all our assets are invested only in a limited number of financial instruments, they are at greater risk than if they included both financial assets and hard assets such as real estate, oil and gas, or collectibles. In terms of diversification, there truly is safety in numbers.

The traditional stock/bond portfolio's diversification is limited to the number of different stock and bond issues purchased for the portfolio. It can be said to be diversified on only one level or plane. The multifund portfolio, by comparison, achieves diversification on three separate and distinct levels. And if we accept the principle that the greater the diversification, the lower the risk and the higher the safety, then a triply diversified portfolio would obviously be the answer to success in a market environment that has become ever more treacherous. Let us call those three levels of diversification the *triple safety net.*

LEVEL ONE: EACH INVESTMENT WITHIN THE PORTFOLIO IS IN ITSELF DIVERSIFIED

Very simply put, if an investor were lazy and purchased only one mutual fund (instead of going to the time and trouble of creating a multifund portfolio), this fact alone would provide the same degree of diversification as the traditional stock/bond portfolio. Each investment in our portfolio is a mutual fund; each mutual fund is a diversified portfolio of stocks and/or bonds. A one-fund portfolio provides similar diversification to (or better diversification than) the traditional portfolio. A portfolio of funds will provide far greater diversification.

LEVEL TWO: DIVERSIFICATION ACROSS A BROADER ARRAY OF ASSET TYPES AND MARKET SECTORS

As stated earlier, a portfolio invested in a single-industry group contains far more risk than one more broadly invested across a wide cross section of the market. Since mutual funds are concentrated portfolios of whichever market sectors or asset types we choose to include in our multifund portfolio, they allow us to capture a far broader assortment of alternatives from the expanded spectrum of investments available today.

If we restudy the fixed-income sector of the model portfolio in the previous chapter (see Figure 14–4), we can focus more sharply on this issue. Instead of looking upon fixed-income funds as a sector of a larger portfolio, we should consider them as a portfolio within themselves. In addition, let us compare this sector to a fixed-income portfolio invested directly in bonds. While the traditional portfolio may contain perhaps as many as 30 to 40 bond issues, it is limited in diversification. Why? Because the

investor or portfolio manager assembling a list of investments may apply a certain point of view over the entire
portfolio. If that individual is optimistic about the future
course of interest rates, he or she will probably invest the
vast majority of holdings in the portfolio in long-maturity
bonds—many of which may be of lower quality. If the
investor is pessimistic about the rate situation, the portfolio may be dominated by shorter-term, higher-grade
issues. In other words, while the portfolio might contain
30 to 40 investments, in reality most of its issues may be
similar to each other.

By comparison, let us look at a fixed-income portfolio
of mutual funds. Keep in mind that we are using the
fixed-income sector of a balanced portfolio. If we were
reviewing the fixed-income sector of a maximum-yield
portfolio, we might be considering seven or eight funds,
instead of four. But the point still comes across. We no
longer have a single investor or portfolio manager dictat-
ing the composition of our bond portfolio. Instead, we
have four portfolio managers making those decisions,
each insulated from the others. So no one prejudice will
affect the overall composition of our fixed-income portfolio. The result is a multifaceted bond portfolio that effectively captures as many different niches within the broad
category called *bonds* as we choose.

Using four carefully selected fixed-income funds, we
can gain exposure to long-term, high-grade bonds; to long-
term, lower-grade bonds; to mixed-grade, mixed-term
bonds; and to intermediate-term bonds. As investors with
a maximum-yield objective, we could have added funds
invested in convertible bonds, deep discount issues, zeros,
Ginnie Maes, or any number of alternatives. The flexibility provided by a multifund portfolio facilitates the efficient representation within a single portfolio of as many
different asset types and market sectors as we choose.
This is an additional form of diversification.

LEVEL THREE: DIVERSIFICATION WITHIN SECTORS BY INVESTMENT STYLE

In Chapter Thirteen we stressed the need to identify clearly each fund candidate's investment style. This allows us to build in the final level of diversification. We are not going to select at random three or four funds that will represent the aggressive-growth sector in our overall portfolio. We will not select a variety of equity-income funds for our multifund portfolio strictly on the basis of their past performance. Instead, we will take the time and effort to define clearly what makes each fund tick and what differentiates it from every other fund in the portfolio, particularly those in the same sector.

As we have said a number of times in this book, investment styles and themes come and go. This level of diversification ensures that a total sector of our portfolio will not underperform because a single investment style has fallen out of favor. Let us assume that our sector allocation to aggressive-growth funds was proved accurate by subsequent market behavior, but that instead of investing in four aggressive-growth funds, we chose only one. If that fund represented a style that was currently out of sync with the investing public's preferences, our entire sector might underperform. This is hardly theoretical. Let us assume that at the beginning of 1984 the balanced investors described in the previous chapter had chosen a high-tech fund for the 25 percent of assets to be invested for aggressive growth. In retrospect, their sector allocation would have proved to be totally accurate, but its performance would have ended up as subpar.

The success or failure of a multifund portfolio is not determined by the investment acumen of one investor or one portfolio manager. Instead, it results from the combined expertise of 10 to 20 different professionals, each of whom has a totally different perspective on investing. Each professional views this amorphous process called stock-and-bond investing from a totally different vantage point. That is the ultimate beauty of the multifund approach. Let us assume that one, two, or three of these managers "bomb out." This should be no surprise since we know that there can never be a situation in which every investment style represented in our portfolio will be in the ascendancy at the same time. Even so, our portfolio as a whole will still succeed. This is because we have 9, 10, 11, or 12 other styles in the portfolio, each of which is managed by professionals with an above average track record. And they can take up the slack. Just think, if our portfolio has just one more winning style than it has styles on the losing side, the whole portfolio will end up as a plus! If there are 14 well-chosen funds in the portfolio—funds with long-term, above average performance histories—and if all of them perform proportionately and only eight of them achieve a gain, the portfolio will still succeed. We will enjoy safe, consistent returns, regardless of the market's direction or our own objective. Why? Because of the triple safety net of multifund investing.

As the investment world becomes more and more volatile and more and more complex, the paramount consideration in any portfolio will be to reduce risk and maximize safety. By providing three separate and distinct levels of diversification, the multifund portfolio has built in the essential characteristics for success in such an environment.

Is multifund investing revolutionary? Perhaps it was revolutionary when first launched in the mid-1970s. But today most people in the pension fund world are investing their assets according to the same principles. Estimates within the investment community are that upward of 70 percent of Fortune 500 companies are using the services of independent pension consultants to assist them with their pension plans.

What, then, is the role of the independent pension consultants? Their duties include the following: (*a*) helping clients to set their investment objectives; (*b*) preparing asset allocation models; and (*c*) performing a search for appropriate managers for the clients' assets. In performing the search for appropriate managers, the independent pension consultants have a number of tasks to carry out:

1. They must do research on the hundreds of independent investment counselors, bank trust departments, common accounts of insurance companies, and others who provide investment management services to pension plans.
2. They must identify the superior performers and their areas of expertise.
3. They must suggest to the plan sponsors a team of managers that can implement the total range of asset allocation developed for a particular plan.

The buzzword for this approach is *multimanager, multistyle investing.* Table 15–1 displays the lineup of managers of some Fortune 500 companies.

In effect, multifund investing provides the same objective setting, the same asset allocation and sector allocation, and the same multimanager, multistyle portfolio structuring as we see in Table 15–1. The only difference is the use of mutual funds in lieu of private account managers. The multifund portfolio enables investors of any size or any level of sophistication to enjoy the benefits of this investment approach. In fact, even those in a position to utilize private account managers are probably better off using multifund investing. This is because of the advantages of mutual funds that were explained

TABLE 15–1 Lineup of Managers of Some
Fortune 500 Companies

AT&T
  Aldrich, Eastman & Waltch, Inc., Boston
  AT&T In-House
  AT&T In-House Coldwell Banker
  AT&T In-House J. W. O'Connor
  AT&T In-House Non S&P Index Fund
  AT&T In-House S&P Index Fund
  AT&T In-House Venture Capital
  David L. Babson & Co., Inc., Boston
  Bankers Trust Company-Investment Management Group, New York
  Batterymarch Financial Management, Boston
  The Boston Company Energy Advisors, Inc., Boston
  The Boston Company Real Estate Counsel, Inc., Boston
  Brown Brothers Harriman & Co., New York
  Capital Guardian Trust Company, Los Angeles
  Chase Investors Management Corporation, New York
  Chemical Bank, New York
  Citibank, N.A., New York
  Denver Investment Advisors, Inc.
  Eastdil Realty Inc., New York
  Equitable Life Assurance Society of the United States, Secaucus
  Favia, Hill & Associates, New York
  Fidelity International Investment Advisors Limited, Boston
  The First National Bank of Atlanta
  The First National Bank of Chicago, Chicago
  G.T. Capital Management, Inc., San Francisco
  Goldman Sachs Realty, New York
  The Griffin Group, Chicago
  Heitman Advisory Corporation, Chicago
  In House Asset Management
  InterFirst Bank Dallas, N.A., Dallas
  Investment Counselors of Maryland, Inc., Baltimore
  Jennison Associates Capital Corporation, New York
  John Hancock Mutual Life Insurance Company, Boston
  Lincoln Capital Management Company, Chicago
  Loomis, Sayles & Company, Inc., Chicago
  Lord, Abbett & Co., New York
  Manufacturers Hanover Investment Corporation, New York
  Mellon Bank Corporation, Pittsburgh
  Mercantile Trust Company, N.A., St. Louis
  Morgan Grenfell Investment Services Limited, London
  J. P. Morgan Investment Management Inc., New York

TABLE 15-1 *(continued)*

AT&T *(continued)*
NCNB National Bank, Charlotte
New England Mutual Life Insurance Company, Boston
Pacific Investment Management Company, Newport Beach
Provident Capital Management, Philadelphia
Provident National Assurance Company, Chattanooga
The Prudential Insurance Company of America through Prudential
    Asset Management Co., Inc., Newark
Rosenberg Capital Management, San Francisco
The RREEF Funds, San Francisco
Seattle-First National Bank, Seattle
Standish, Ayer & Wood, Inc., Boston
State Street Bank & Trust Company, Boston
State Street Research & Management Company, Boston
Thorndike, Doran, Paine & Lewis, Boston
United Capital Management, Denver
United States Trust Company of New York
Wachovia Bank & Trust Company, N.A., Winston-Salem
Wells Fargo Bank, San Francisco
Western Asset Management Company, Los Angeles

General Motors Corporation
Aldrich, Eastman & Waltch, Inc., Boston
American National Bank and Trust Company of Chicago
AmeriTrust Company, Cleveland
Bank of America, San Francisco
Bankers Trust Company-Investment Management Group, New York
Baring International Investment Limited, Boston
The Boston Company, Inc., Boston
The Boston Company Real Estate Counsel, Inc., Boston
Capital Guardian Trust Company, Los Angeles
The Chase Manhattan Bank, New York
Citibank, N.A., New York
Daiwa International Capital Management Corp., New York
Dimensional Fund Advisors, Inc., Santa Monica
Fidelity International Investment Advisors Limited, Boston
Fidelity Management Trust Company, Boston
First National Bank of Boston
The First National Bank of Chicago, Chicago
G.T. Capital Management, Inc., San Francisco
Harris Trust and Savings Bank, Chicago
In House Asset Management

TABLE 15–1 *(continued)*

General Motors Corporation *(continued)*
 InterFirst Bank Dallas, N.A., Dallas
 INVESCO Capital Management, Inc., Atlanta
 Jennison Associates Capital Corporation, New York
 Kleinwort Benson International Investment Ltd., New York
 Landauer Advisors, Inc., New York
 Lincoln Capital Management Company, Chicago
 Mellon Bank Corporation, Pittsburgh
 Metropolitan Life Insurance Company, New York
 J. P. Morgan Investment Management Inc., New York
 National Bank of Detroit
 Nomura Capital Management, Inc., New York
 Rowe Price-Fleming International, Inc., Baltimore
 N. M. Rothschild International Asset Management Ltd., London
 Schroder Capital Management International, Inc., New York
 TCW Asset Management Company, Los Angeles
 United Capital Management, Denver
 Weiss, Peck & Greer, New York
 Wells Fargo Bank, San Francisco
 Wells Fargo Investment Advisors, San Francisco
 Wells Fargo Realty Advisors, San Francisco
 ACTUARY: The Wyatt Company
 SEARCH CONSULTANT: Frank Russell Company, Institutional Data
  Division, Tacoma

Salaried Retirement Program (noninsured portion)
 Aldrich, Eastman & Waltch, Inc., Boston
 American National Bank and Trust Company of Chicago
 AmeriTrust Company, Cleveland
 Bank of America, San Francisco
 Bankers Trust Company-Investment Management Group, New York
 Baring International Investment Limited, Boston
 The Boston Company, Inc., Boston
 The Boston Company Real Estate Counsel, Inc., Boston
 Capital Guardian Trust Company, Los Angeles
 The Chase Manhattan Bank, New York
 Citibank, N.A., New York
 Daiwa International Capital Management Corp., New York
 Dimensional Fund Advisors, Inc., Santa Monica
 Fidelity International Investment Advisors Limited, Boston
 First National Bank of Boston
 The First National Bank of Chicago, Chicago
 G. T. Capital Management, Inc., San Francisco

TABLE 15–1 *(continued)*

General Motors Corporation *(continued)*
  Harris Trust and Savings Bank, Chicago
  In House Asset Management
  InterFirst Bank Dallas, N.A., Dallas
  Invesco Capital Management, Inc., Atlanta
  Jennison Associates Capital Corporation, New York
  Kleinwort Benson International Investment Ltd., New York
  Landauer Advisors, Inc., New York
  Lincoln Capital Management Company, Chicago
  Mellon Bank Corporation, Pittsburgh
  Metropolitan Life Insurance Company, New York
  J. P. Morgan Investment Management Inc., New York
  National Bank of Detroit
  Nomura Capital Management, Inc., New York
  Rowe Price-Fleming International, Inc., Baltimore
  N. M. Rothschild International Asset Management Ltd., London
  Schroder Capital Management International, Inc., New York
  TCW Asset Management Company, Los Angeles
  United Capital Management, Denver
  Weiss, Peck & Greer, New York
  Wells Fargo Bank, San Francisco

SOURCE: T. H. Fitzgerald, Jr., ed., *Directory of Pension Funds and Their Investment Managers—1986* (Charlottesville, VA: Money Market Directories, Inc., 1986), pp. 810 and 830.

in Chapters Six and Seven when we compared this approach to the inefficiencies of individual private accounts. Besides, most major investment management firms serving the world of tax-exempt plans also have publicly available mutual funds that offer exactly the same investment expertise. Included are such firms as Delaware Investment Advisors–Delaware Funds, Capital Guardian Trust–American Funds, and Fidelity Trust–Fidelity Funds.

Let us summarize here. For individual investors and sponsors of smaller plans, multifund investing provides access to the same state-of-the-art investment thinking as heretofore was only available to sponsors of large plans. It allows bank trust departments and investment counseling firms to offer clients a comprehensive approach by providing through one source what would otherwise only be available through a team of managers. It provides sponsors of large plans with access to the same investment expertise they are probably receiving through their present manager lineup, but in a far more efficient fashion.

WHAT ABOUT THE DANGER OF OVERDIVERSIFICATION?

At this point, we need to answer a question that has been raised about overdiversification. A number of studies have concluded that diversification to reduce risk works only up to a certain point. It is generally believed that—so far as stock portfolios are concerned—the maximum benefit accrues in a portfolio of 30 to 40 stocks. Beyond that number, according to these studies, there seems to be no perceptible advantage to diversification in most cases. (Perhaps this occurs because of the unwieldiness of broadly based portfolios—a development we mentioned in Chapter Two.) So the question arises whether a multi-fund portfolio that indirectly invests in hundreds of stocks and bonds might not be overdiversified.

Our answer is no. The studies on the maximum level of efficient diversification are probably correct, but they apply only when direct investments are made in stocks and bonds. This is because too many issues in a portfolio place too much of a strain on the portfolio manager. A portfolio with 60 to 75 stocks demands too much time and attention. But a multifund portfolio contains only 10 to 20 funds that have to be followed. There is no strain, and there is no "washing out" (because an overdiversified portfolio may have as many losers as winners). Because of the efficiency of multifund investing, we can enjoy the benefits of broad diversification without suffering any negative effects. As Solveig Jansson wrote in 1978, this investment approach is not overdiversification but "superdiversification."[1]

WHAT ABOUT INDEXING?

A second question concerns indexing. As we said earlier, many investors who feel despair over their inability to "beat the market" have turned to indexing. This means buying a group of stocks or bonds in direct proportion to their representation in a broad market index, such as the Standard & Poor's 500 Stock Average, the Dow Jones Industrial Average, or the Shearson/Lehman Bond Index. As a result, these investors hope that their investments will always approximate those of "the market" as represented by one of those indexes. Since a multifund portfolio captures so many different market sectors, is it really no more than a superindex fund?

To reply to this question, we need to point out that indexing implies a goal of matching market returns by creating a market portfolio. Multifund investing does not seek market returns. By investing in mutual funds with consistent, above average performance, the goal is to achieve market returns plus. The total number of market niches represented in the portfolio is immaterial. If we were to purchase within each sector an index fund, the claim would be true that a multifund portfolio is no more than a superindex fund. But this is not the case. In each sector we invest in funds with above average records. The cumulative effect, then, is that as long as more than half of the funds selected perform up to expectations or histori-

---

[1]Solveig Jansson, "Portfolio Strategy," *Institutional Investor Magazine*, December 1978.

cal norms, we have at a minimum created a superindex fund plus. This is exactly what every investor wants!

This is the essence of multifund investing, its conceptual strengths, its practical aspects, and its inherent advantages. All that remains now is for us to explain how to keep the multifund portfolio on track and how to make sure it meets our expectations as time goes on.

How to Keep a Portfolio Current

Multifund investing is a live process; it is not something carried out once and then forgotten. Even though it reduces a significant portion of the time required to manage a portfolio, some upkeep is still required. Our situation as investors may change, economic and political settings may shift, stock and bond market environments may go through ebbs and flows. All these changes require us to reevaluate our portfolio.

When we first diagrammed and outlined the pyramid-like, four-step process of constructing a multifund portfolio in Chapter Eight, we said this was a top-down approach. At the time we were referring to the process of creating a portfolio. But now we are referring to portfolio maintenance. *Changes at any level of the pyramid automatically require changes on all lower levels.* If our objective changes, the asset allocation, sector allocation, and mutual fund selection must all be adjusted. If our asset allocation changes, sector allocation and mutual fund selection must be modified. If our sector allocation is altered, mutual fund selection must be shifted.

Modifications are definitely not from the bottom up. Different mutual funds can be selected without affecting our sector allocation, asset allocation, or objective. Sector allocation can be reformulated without any effect on our asset allocation and objective. Asset allocation can be shifted without changing our objective. That is why we call this a top-down approach, both in terms of original structuring as well as of subsequent modifications. How those adjustments are accomplished and what sort of circumstances precipitate these changes will be the focus of this chapter.

CHANGES IN OBJECTIVE

There are any number of reasons why we might want to change our objective or goal. For instance, our financial situation might change. There might be a change in our job that leads to a substantial increase in salary and more income becoming available for investments. We might receive a large inheritance. If our investments are associated with a retirement plan, a sudden rise in the number of retirees might occur, or an important source of income, might suddenly be cut off. In all these cases our perception of the purpose of the pool of assets in our investment account—whether it be to generate current income or to develop long-term capital appreciation—will change. Of necessity, this new development will trigger changes in all the steps that follow. Whether we place increased emphasis on capital appreciation at the expense of current income, or vice versa, the existing allocations to growth-oriented investments, income-oriented investments, and liquid investments will have to be shifted. In turn, this will force changes in sector allocation and mutual fund selection. Let us assume, for example, that circumstances may dictate a change in objective from maximum yield to maximum growth—admittedly a radical shift, but one that is quite possible. In the past we may have not made any allocations either to aggressive-growth funds or even to conservative-growth funds. But our new objective may now dictate placing a considerable emphasis on those sectors and on the funds needed to fill those slots.

Another factor that might alter our objective pertains to a shift in our life cycle. To wit, the original purpose of our investment account might have been to fund our children's college expenses. When they graduate, changes may have to be made. You will recall that in the model used in Chapter Fourteen, the original goal of that couple was to amass a pool of capital for retirement. When retirement eventually arrives, that couple may go from a balanced objective to a maximum yield objective. Or consider a young, high-earning professional investing for maximum growth who marries and has children. That investor's objective might shift to either growth or a balanced objective. In turn, the asset and sector allocations of those investors would have to be adjusted, and their mutual fund selection shifted accordingly.

Age alone may often play a role. A 40-year-old may be in a relatively similar financial situation to the one he or she was in at 30, but that person's temperament may have become more conservative. The same thing might happen when we pass from middle age to the role of senior citizens. As our temperament or outlook on life changes, so, too, our investment objectives may alter. Tied into both the life cycle and considerations of age is a general sense of risk-aversion. Usually as we age, or as our responsibilities increase or decrease, our aversion to risk will shift. As Table 9–1 on page 120 pointed out, there is a definite correlation between objective and risk level. Therefore, a new outlook on risk-aversion will force a change in our objective. This change will then affect our asset allocation, our sector allocation, and our mutual fund selection.

CHANGES IN ASSET ALLOCATION

Let us consider the following scenario: the economy has passed its high point and seems to be sliding toward a recession. The money supply is growing rapidly, and fears are increasing that the Federal Reserve Board will force interest rates higher. The stock market has risen 30 percent in a matter of months and now seems overpriced on a price/earnings basis. The U.S. Congress is considering bills that will eradicate the budget deficit, which should spur economic growth.

These kinds of developments affecting the economy, money supply, investment market, and political situation ought to trigger a modification in our asset allocation. Events or trends construed as positive for economic expansion would trigger increases in our allocation to growth. Developments with negative implication for the economy would call for a reduction in the growth allocation and a commensurate increase in either income or liquid investments. Trends construed as significantly detrimental for interest rates would probably result in a decrease in our income allocation and an increase in our liquid investments. Conversely, signs of sharply lower interest rates would call for a reallocation from liquid to income investments.

Once these reallocations are made, they automatically cause reallocations among sectors. For instance, if the commitment to growth assets is reduced, commensurate reductions will have to be made in either the allocation to the aggressive-growth sector, the conservative-growth sector, or both. Thereafter, changes will be forced in the allocations to individual aggressive-growth funds and conservative-growth funds.

CHANGES IN SECTOR ALLOCATION

Changes like those described above that may affect the economy, money supply, investment market, and political situation may also require us to adjust our sector allocation. The difference is a matter of degree. Events or developments with a significant impact would cause a modification in our asset allocation. Those of minor import would leave our asset allocation intact, but trigger an adjustment in our sector allocation.

For instance, if a stock market rally was still in progress, but we felt that the major part of the advance had already taken place, our allocation to growth investments might remain the same. But on the sector level we might want to shift assets from aggressive-growth funds to conservative-growth funds. Similarly, when interest rates continue to fall but appear ready to level off, our allocation to income-oriented investments can remain intact. But we may well want to shift our assets from long-term bond funds to intermediate-term funds (or more subtly yet, from lower-graded bond funds to higher-grade funds).

Thereafter, the type and number of funds used would have to be adjusted. If our portfolio had had a 50 percent allocation to growth funds, of which 25 percent was in aggressive-growth funds and 25 percent in conservative-growth funds, we might now adjust this allocation to 5 percent in aggressive-growth funds and 45 percent in conservative-growth funds. As a result, the number of aggressive funds might shrink from four to one, while the list of conservative funds might expand from three to four or five. Alternatively, the same number of funds might be used in a different situation, but the percentage allocation to each fund might be reduced or increased. This is the chain-reaction effect of adjusting our sector allocation.

CHANGES IN MUTUAL FUND SELECTION

Let us now go to a new scenario. We will assume that there is no change in our objective as investors nor are there any changes in our asset allocation or sector allocation. Still there might be four important reasons for us to alter the composition of our portfolio in terms of the selection of mutual funds.

A Change in Portfolio Managers. In many cases a fund's good performance record can be directly attributed to the investment talents of a single individual in the fund's management. If that individual leaves the employ of the fund, and if a review of the successor's talents leaves us somewhat uneasy, we should probably drop that particular fund. Its attractiveness is often due entirely to the investment professional who was running it. As we noted in discussing the personalization test in Chapter Thirteen, if we purchase a fund strictly on the basis of its past performance and are unaware that the individual primarily responsible for such good results is no longer associated with the fund, this is like buying a pig in a poke.

Variation in Performance.   No matter how fine our screening process may have been, a fund's fortunes can unexpectedly take a turn for the worse for an extended period—say, longer than 12 months. The same professionals are in charge, and the same investment style is being implemented, but suddenly the fund no longer performs up to expectations. If we as investors are not prepared to "weather the storm," the fund should be dropped.

Alteration in Investment Style.   Occasionally—but fortunately rarely—something goes haywire with fund managers, and they may no longer adhere to their past investment style. One case in particular comes to mind. An aggressive growth fund that had performed exceptionally well for a number of years suddenly fell to the very depths of performance. This fund had a regimented investment policy whereby the fund's assets would be invested in stocks whose recent price action was stronger than that of other stocks. (This is often called *relative strength policy*.) In the early 1980s this policy resulted in a heavy concentration in the portfolio of oil stocks, which had resulted in the previous superior performance. As the fund's performance started to slip, I had occasion to visit the portfolio manager. In reviewing his portfolio, I noticed that it was still heavily weighted with the oil stocks. Even the most casual stock market observer could have realized that those stocks could not be highly ranked on any scale of relative strength. I inquired in particular about Kirby Oil, the fund's single largest position. The fund manager's response was something like this: "No, Kirby no longer appears on the top of the relative strength list, but I've grown to know the company very well, and it continues to be a good buy." A wise observer once remarked about the danger of "falling in love with one's own investments" or "getting smarter than the system." Lack of discipline can result in an emotional involvement with a fund or in scrapping tried and proved investment methods for the sake of novelty. Such mistakes can be the undoing of even the most astute investors. Any indication of this malaise would be an immediate cause for us to cease investing in that particular fund.

Substitution of a Preferred Alternate. Occasionally we may decide to make a change in our portfolio for still another reason. For example, we may have purchased a certain fund in order to capture a particular niche or investment style. But additional screening of funds in that same category may uncover another fund whose performance record is equally good or perhaps better in coverage of the same niche or sector. A personalization test we conduct may reinforce the attractiveness of the alternate. Even though the fund currently in our portfolio continues to perform to our expectation, we may decide to substitute the alternative fund.

These are typical situations in which we might reformulate the core group of our funds. Notice that no mention is made of dropping funds when they reach a sell point or when they become overvalued. The reason is that no such terminology or concept is applicable to mutual funds. Open-ended, actively managed fund portfolios never reach a sell point or some price at which they are seen as overvalued. If the portfolio manager remains the same, if the investment philosophy and policies of the fund continue intact, the shares can be retained. A fund has no price/earnings ratio (the standard barometer by which we determine a sell point or by which a stock is determined to become overvalued). This is because the implied price/earnings ratio is in a constant state of flux as underlying stocks are bought and sold. If the portfolio is properly managed—selling securities that deserve to be sold and buying suitable replacements—then its implied price/earnings multiple can never get too "rich."

* * *

FIGURE 16–1 How Changes at Any Level of the Investment Pyramid Require Changes at All the Lower Levels

If the _____ changes, then the _____ must be adjusted	
Objective	Asset allocation, sector allocation, and mutual fund selection
Asset allocation	Sector allocation and mutual fund selection
Sector allocation	Mutual fund selection
Mutual fund selection	Individual mutual funds

We can sum up easily the conclusions reached in this chapter by means of Figure 16–1.

If we pay careful attention to the suggestions in this chapter, we will change our objectives when such action is called for. We will adjust our asset allocation and sector allocation as conditions require us to do so. And we will alter, when necessary, the mix of our funds. By following this procedure, we will make certain that our multifund portfolio continues to deliver the results we expect from it.

CHAPTER SEVENTEEN

A Summary

Since the early 1970s the investment markets have experienced a number of significant changes. Volatility and complexity have so altered the nature of the markets that the traditional methods of investing through broadly diversified portfolios of stocks or bonds have been unable to achieve the investors' objectives. Because of volatility portfolios must now be adjusted over a far shorter period of time. Because of complexity portfolio managers have to absorb critical information over a much wider spectrum. Since these changes have occurred almost simultaneously, the problem has been exacerbated even further.

We have explored the inherent strengths of the open-ended mutual fund as a potential solution to these problems. Since mutual funds provide what in effect is instant liquidity along with an extremely compact and flexible investment vehicle, investors can cope with volatility. In view of the new dimensions of the fund industry, which offers over 1,300 non–money market, stock, and bond funds, investors are now provided with a range and depth of expertise unmatched by other potential avenues. The entire range of investment alternatives from the most mundane conservative-growth stocks to the most exotic option strategies and medical technology can be captured through one or more funds. Combined, these two major characteristics of mutual funds—their liquidity and the depth of coverage they provide—make them perfect investment vehicles for a volatile, complex market.

Next we took the concept a step further into multifund investing. Instead of considering the purchase of a single fund or a randomly selected group of funds to achieve our objective, we described the following simple four-step process by which we could create a cohesive multifund portfolio of 10 to 20 funds:

1. **Objective Setting.** This means obtaining a clear understanding of an investor's goals as well as of his or her ability to absorb risk.

2. **Asset Allocation.** On the basis of our investor's objective, we consider how various factors, such as developments in the economy, the political situation, the monetary situation, and the market, might affect investments over the next 9 to 15 months. We then develop a plan for deploying the investor's assets among growth, income, and liquid investments.

3. **Sector Allocation.** This involves adding detail to the portfolio matrix by further defining how we are to deploy the assets. We further determine whether growth-oriented assets should be invested in aggressive-growth or conservative-growth funds; whether the income assets should be invested in equity-income funds or fixed-income funds; and finally what type of money market funds should be utilized for liquid investments.

4. **Mutual Fund Selection.** We learn that there is a wrong way and a right way to carry out mutual fund selection. The wrong way is to pursue high-flyers and passing fads while the right way is to identify consistent funds that have been above average in performance. We need to go beyond the historical performance numbers in order to understand the unique characteristics of those funds, such as the investment style and philosophy of their managers. We should then assemble a group of complementary styles and philosophies in a single portfolio so as to provide our investor with the maximum in safety and consistency.

Lastly, we have delved further into the reasons why multifund investing has been able to deliver consistent returns over such an extended time period, regardless of the investor's objective and the market environment. We conclude that a multifund portfolio provides three distinct layers of diversification, the following triple safety net:

1. Each investment within the portfolio is itself diversified.
2. A far greater diversification than the traditional stock and bond portfolio is achieved in the portfolio by capturing many more asset types and market sectors.
3. Within each sector we can achieve a third layer of diversification by investing in a cross section of funds with distinct, complementary investment styles. As a result, no one investment bias or school of thought determines the success or failure of the portfolio. Instead, we can draw on the combined, but totally independent investment expertise of 10 to 20 full-time professionals.

As the investment markets become increasingly volatile and complex, the treacherous aspects of stock and bond investing will increase, while the overriding advantages and safety features of multifund investing should become more important to the investing public. At first thought multifund investing may appear too radical a change in direction for traditionalists to accept. But the record of success of multifund investing speaks for itself. Its ability to deliver what other approaches cannot requires a serious consideration by all investors, regardless of their level of sophistication.

INDEX